TWILIGHT LANGUAGE

A Compendium of the World
of
COIL

by
Edward Pandemonium

HORNGATE

First edition published by
Horngate Media
New Port Richey, FL 34653
USA

ISBN: 978-0-9909700-8-8

Book Layout & Pre-Press:
Philip H. Farber
http://www.hawkridgeproductions.com

Cover Design:
Fergal Fitzpatrick
http://www.fergalfitzpatrick.com

Original drawing by Gareth Jackson

"You have to burn in order to shine." - Coil

ANSWERS COME IN DREAMS

In the summer of 2004 e.v., I had a dream about John (or Jhon) Balance of Coil. He was up on a scaffold, working on stained glass murals of angels. I do not recall exactly how or why but he fell to his death and I was so upset that I awoke, still feeling the physical residuum of the emotion. A few months later, of course, he did fall from a balcony in his home and died as a result. Nine summers later, I awoke from another sleep with the fully-formed intention and plan for doing a book on Coil.

However, this was never going to be a conventional sort of music book that looked at the ordinary facts and trivia of biography, history and discography. No, there are others much more qualified to write such books if they wish to do so. As a Magician, my purpose was going to be re-creating and expanding upon Coil's magical impact.

For me, as a young man first coming into contact with Coil and then relying upon them for much of my life's soundtrack over the decades since, what touched me so profoundly and what I responded to so enthusiastically about the "Coil Experience" was two-fold in nature. The first aspect is perfectly summarized by the following quote:

"Like Burroughs, or Spare, there's no difference between our philosophy, our lifestyle and our art. This is what we do. We are what we do." - John Balance

Coil was real. Their relationships to the ideas, practices, people, places and substances described in this book were not a pose, show or stage theatrics.

The second, related aspect was the diversity of influences and references woven into their work. That is what this book highlights: Coil as occultural nexus. Coil was a repository for ALL of the Arts - arcane and aesthetic - brought together from hidden temples, great museums and the alternative underground, then synthesized through ecstatic ritual and technological innovation to unleash an outpouring of Angels and Abominations, Gold and Sewage, Sex and Death, Matter and Spirit in a totality of Chaos and Dream.

In a sense, the book is an "outagraph" - a Surrealist technique in which the central subject of a photograph is removed, highlighting the space which the subject occupied and the matrix or context surrounding that space. Coil is not here, just as John Balance and Peter Christopherson are no longer here, and the emphasis is shifted to the imaginal world from which their music came forth.

I have tried to expand the scope of the book beyond my own shared interests - my own vision or experience of Coil - but will surely have left out something(s) that other Coil enthusiasts will miss. It would probably be impossible to really include EVERYTHING relevant to such a body of work.

Many of Coil's fans are true fanatics. Following the deaths of Balance and Christopherson, rare items command very high prices at auction. For those who resonated with them, Coil were undoubtedly a magical force. Their songs, albums and (eventual) performances were undoubtedly magical operations.

For my own purposes now, I am reminded that Aleister Crowley said the same thing about books. As he put it:

"It is my Will to inform the World of certain facts within my knowledge. I therefore take 'magical weapons', pen, ink, and paper; I write 'incantations' - these sentences - in the 'magical language' i.e. that which is understood by the people I wish to instruct; I call forth 'spirits', such as printers, publishers, booksellers, and so forth, and constrain them to convey my message to those people. The composition and distribution of this book is thus an act of MAGICK by which I cause

Changes to take place in conformity with my Will."

So, what is my Will?

My Will is to provide everyone from the long-time fan to the complete neophyte with a deeper understanding of Coil's music and thus, hopefully, a deeper experience and appreciation of the work.

Moreover, though, my deeper Will is to demonstrate what Coil were as a way of making Art and doing Magic so that more Artists and Magicians might take up this way in their own manner.

Going back to those days when I first encountered Coil, I remember how certain albums or books could change lives and nourish subcultures. It is an ambitious Wish but I hope that this book can thus act as a source of dual inspiration to new generations so as to keep the DREAM going, growing and evolving.

CHAOS IN EXTENSION

Edward Pandemonium

February 23, 2015 e.v. (Year L AES)

"God grant that the reader, emboldened and having become at present as fierce as what he is reading, find, without loss of bearings, his way, his wild and treacherous passage through the desolate swamps of these sombre, poison-soaked pages; for, unless he should bring to his reading a rigorous logic and a sustained mental effort at least as strong as his distrust, the lethal fumes of this book shall dissolve his soul as water does sugar."

- the Comte de Lautréamont

A

Æ · Pen-name of Irish poet, painter, nationalist and Theosophist George William Russell. Russell worked for the Irish Agricultural Organisation Society (IAOS), both as an organizer and as editor of the *Irish Homestead* journal. He was also editor of the Irish Dominion League's *Irish Statesman* newspaper, which later merged with *Irish Homestead*. Russell also further explicated his political views in novels such as *The Avatars: A Futurist Fantasy*.

On the other hand, as Æ (or AE, an initial for "Aeon"), Russell was a leader of the Hermetic Society and prone to waking dreams or clairvoyant visions of otherworldly realms and beings. These visions provided inspiration for his paintings and are discussed in detail in his book *The Candle of Vision*. In this, Russell might be thought of as something of an Irish, more pagan William Blake.

George Russell's marriage of his nature mysticism with his mundane, practical activities is something rarely seen. Whether or not one shares his particular vision and beliefs, this seamless melding of worlds is a worthy subject of study and emulation for any Magician.

See AVATAR and WILLIAM BLAKE.

EILEEN AGAR · British artist born in Argentina to a Scottish father and American mother. When the family moved to England, little Eileen was accompanied on ship by a cow and an orchestra because her mother believed that fresh milk and good music were essential to her well-being. It probably did not then require much adjustment when she later began associating with Surrealists after studying art in London and Paris.

In addition to paintings, Agar made objects such as the exquisite "Angel of Anarchy" - a bust wrapped in African bark cloth, blindfolded with a Chinese silk sash and adorned with beads, osprey and ostrich feathers and a diamanté nose.

See ANGEL, FETISHISM and SURREALISM.

ALCHEMY - The term Alchemy commonly refers to an occult form of chemistry aimed at producing a universal medicine, an elixir of immortality or for transmuting base metals into gold. By extension, any method of transforming or upgrading substances, relationships, environments or aspects of life or being may be metaphorically (or not metaphorically) referred to as Alchemy.

We might think of Alchemy as being first and foremost a worldview and approach to existence and that its art, science and processes derive from that approach and the application of that worldview. In his essential work on the subject, *The Forge and the Crucible*, Mircea Eliade tells us:

"Alchemy has bequeathed much more to the modern world than a rudimentary chemistry; it has left us its faith in the transmutation of Nature and its ambition to control Time."

For example, it was believed among ancient Chinese alchemists that there were two kinds of Immortality Pill. The first was naturally occuring. This would be a mineral or stone that has fortuitously absorbed just the right balance of alternating *yang* and *yin* essences, being exposed to the exactly correct amounts of sunlight and moonlight over a period of 4,320 years. Such pills are going to be extremely rare and difficult to find, so the task of the alchemist is to understand these processes and then to intentionally replicate them over a much shorter span of time.

The alchemists of Europe had similar ideas concerning the evolution or maturation of metals through time; that gold had passed through stages of being mercury, copper, lead and so on over the course of its incredibly long existence and that this process could be accelerated in the laboratory.

Legends do tell of alchemists becoming immortal and successfully making gold but these are not confirmed facts. Because the world is not overrun with Immortals and mountains of gold, we are inclined to assume that either their theories or technology were inadequate to the task. However, the newer theories and upgraded processes of modern science have turned mercury and bismuth to gold in the laboratory and show great promise in the radical extension of lifespan. On the strictly physical level, Alchemy, itself, appears to have been alchemized.

However, in another essential alchemical text, Israel Regardie's *The Philosopher's Stone*, three non-physical theories of Alchemy are put forward: the Psychological, the "Magnetic" or Energetic and the Magical. Being both a practitioner of the psychological and energetic therapy of Wilhelm Reich and a student of the magical systems of the Hermetic Order of the Golden Dawn and Aleister Crowley, Regardie was familiar with all three and *The Philosopher's Stone* is recommended. However, those looking to go deeper into the psychological approach would do well to also study the related writings of Carl Gustav Jung and his student Marie-Louise von Franz, while those interested in the energetic approach should look to the Daoist practice called *Neidan*. A combination of both approaches would be good.

The magical approach is not so well-known, though it is perhaps the thread that runs through the whole of this book that you hold. It certainly combines the psychological and energetic views of Alchemy along with those aims described by Eliade above - which are, indeed, the aims of Magic, as well. Magical ritual engages and unites all of the media of the Self: all parts of the mind and brain, all of the senses, the actions of the body and even the design of one's environment into a whole and integrated expression of the Will. It also requires the creation of magical artifacts. The material stuff and substance of the world is transformed though ritual just as space and time are.

And so, Magic and Alchemy overlap and co-evolve.

See BLACK SUN, MAX ERNST, HIEROGLYPHIC MONAD, GOLD, SIR EDWARD KELLEY, MERCURY, SCATOLOGY, SURREALISM and TWILIGHT LANGUAGE.

MARC ALMOND · Originally "Peter Mark Sinclair Almond", Marc Almond is an English singer, songwriter and musician, active in Soft Cell (with Dave Ball), Marc and the Marimbas, a solo career and a wide variety of collaborations with other artists. Probably best known for Soft Cell's covers of "Tainted Love" (Gloria Jones) and "Where Did Our Love Go?" (The Supremes), as well as his own "Tears Run Rings". Be on the lookout for Soft Cell's truly magical "Sex Dwarf" video.

He has also put out a number of books, such as the poetry collection *The Angel of Death in the Adonis Lounge* and his autobiography, *Tainted Life*.

In 2012 e.v., Almond played the role of Seneca, the Greek Stoic philosopher, in an adaptation of Claudio Monteverdi's opera *The Coronation of Poppea* staged at the Théâtre du Châtelet in Paris.

See BOYD RICE and MARIMBA.

AMETHYST DECEIVER · A small, edible mushroom (*Laccaria amethystina*) named for its vivid, purple color. Found in temperate climates around the world. Its color fades with age.

AMPHETAMINE · Powerful stimulant of the central nervous system. Amphetamines have been used in medicine to treat asthma, narcolepsy and hyperactivity. Because of their performance enhancing qualities such as increased alertness and motivation, amphetamines were used extensively by soldiers and pilots on both sides of the Second

World War. The Nazis had, in fact, tested a drug cocktail called D-IX that combined methamphetamine with cocaine and oxycodone and enabled equipment-laden subjects to march for over fifty miles before collapsing in exhaustion. Today, amphetamines are often used by students or others similarly working to mental deadlines.

See MDMA.

ANALOGUE SYNTHESIS - The sound synthesizers of today are, of course, digital and create and process sounds as a series of numbers. However, the early synthesizers used to produce electronic music were developed from assorted pieces of electronic equipment such as amplifiers, filters, oscillators, signal generators and so on that were continuous rather than binary (digital) in their variability of signal. One early synthesizer, the Trautonium (c. 1929 e.v.), was played by using a finger to glide a resistor wire over a metal plate. Volume was controlled by pressure.

The first synthesizers consisted of a large number of modules that could be connected together in any way desired. These set-ups could be quite large, even taking up whole walls. Later units consisting of only a few key modules with a standard connection and an attached keyboard sacrificed such flexibility for portability, but greatly contributed to the proliferation of electronic music in doing so.

See ANS SYNTHESIZER, GRANULAR SYNTHESIS and INDUSTRIAL CULTURE.

ANGEL - From the Greek *aggelos* or "messenger". Most commonly known from the Abrahamic religions, where angels are supernatural beings that serve Jehovah/Allah as extensions of his will. For example, the angel Gabriel who informed Mary of her Immaculate Conception in Christianity is also the angel Jibril who revealed the Quran to Muhamad.

However, there is also much lore of angels who were disobedient or "fallen", such as those described in Genesis 6:1-4 of the Bible and the apocryphal Book of Enoch. These "Sons of God" or "Watchers" are said to have fathered the Nephilimic races upon human women.

More famously, Satan, the ruler of Hell, is said to have formerly been the greatest of angels, who rebelled against Jehovah and instigated War in Heaven. Cast out, his fallen fellows became demons along with him and angels no more. Another legend says that the Fairy Folk of Celtic lands were once also angels, those who remained neutral in the Great War and thus came to dwell upon Earth.

Comparable entities, the *Yazatas* and *Amesha Spentas* can be found in Zoroastrianism. These names mean "Worthy of Veneration" and "Bounteous Immortals" respectively. The former lends itself to the term Yazdanism, which describes several Kurdish sects that venerate such beings. This includes the Yazidis, who are often (and perhaps inaccurately) called "devil-worshippers" for their veneration of the Peacock Angel, *Melek Taus*.

In addition to religious history, angels also have a prominent place in magical history. Indeed, the aforementioned Watchers are said in the Book of Enoch to have taught Magic along with other arts and sciences to the human women that they took as lovers and their children. Azazel taught metallurgy, the forging of weapons and the use of cosmetics. Semyaza taught enchantments and root-cuttings, while Armaros taught the resolution of enchantments and still others taught the lore of weather and of the stars and planets.

In the magical systems based upon the seven classical planets, each has a ruling angel of its own and the magical systems developed by Dr. John Dee are said to have been dictated by the angels, themselves - even partially in their own language. Even more orthodox practices such as praying to Archangels or Guardian Angels may be considered part of this magical stream.

This is especially so with regard to the Guardian Angel, which may be seen by Magicians as akin to the personal *Daimon* of the ancient Greeks or the Roman *Genius*. In his seminal statement of Renaissance

Humanism, Giovanni Pico della Mirandola argues that because Man differs from all other animals in having no implicit nature or function, he may become what he wills to become and should thus strive to emulate the angels. The famous grimoire *The Book of the Sacred Magic of Abramelin the Mage* describes how one might obtain "knowledge and conversation" of one's own Holy Guardian Angel, who will reveal magical secrets. The Thelemic system of Aleister Crowley combines these ideas, making such knowledge and conversation the key to spiritual attainment and the discovery of one's True Will (which may or may not be a contradiction of Pico's position described above).

Crowley's conception of the Holy Guardian Angel and True Will may be even further enhanced for the contemporary Magician by Roberto Assagioli's writings on the Superconscious Self and the machinery of Will in his system known as Psychosynthesis.

See EILEEN AGAR, WILLIAM BLAKE, DEATH, SIR JOHN DEE, ESCHATON, SIR EDWARD KELLEY, MARS, MERCURY, MOON, THELEMA and VULTURE.

ANS SYNTHESIZER · The ANS synthesizer was created by a Russian engineer named Evgeny Murzin over a period from 1937 to 1957 e.v. It was named for the Russian composer, occultist, pianist and possible synesthesist Alexander Nikolayevich Scriabin (ANS), who related sound and color to each other in his work.

The ANS works along the same lines as the technology used in creating optical soundtracks on film · but in reverse. With the ANS, drawings are made upon a glass plate and then photoelectronically converted to sound. The plate can be scanned left or right and at varying speeds.

See ANALOGUE SYNTHESIS and SYNESTHESIA.

ANTICHRIST · In the New Testament of the Bible, the term "antichrist" is used to collectively describe those who deny the existence of the flesh-and-blood Jesus as the "Son of God". In later use, and especially today, the two Beasts and False Prophet of the Book of the Apocalypse or Revelation are conflated into a composite end-times tyrant who is a pawn or even incarnation of Satan and referred to as the (singular) Antichrist.

Comparable figures also exist in Judaism and Islam. For medieval Jews, the anti-Messiah *Armilus* is an oppressor who will conquer Jerusalem and persecute the Jews until being destroyed by the true Messiah or directly by Jehovah. For the Muslims, *al-Masih ad-Dajjal*, the Deceiving Messiah, is one who will appear and impersonate the true Messiah. While Armilus is said to be partially maimed and leprous, ad-Dajjal is said to be blind in one eye.

But if the Antichrist is a counterfeit and Great Deceiver of the masses as is so often said, there are issues that we must consider. Those Gnostic sects which distinguish the Christ ("Anointed") spirit from Jesus as a man - and thus considered antichrists, themselves, according to orthodoxy as described above - held that the Christ was a liberating spirit opposed to the *Demiurge* or Master of this World and its servants, the *Archons* ("Rulers"), who work to keep souls in ignorance and bondage.

If we consider the Christ in this sense, we must ask: What has been the oppressor of the Spirit? What has been the suppressor of knowledge? What has shed the blood of countless men, women and children in tyranny? And yet...who has been mindlessly adored as an idol by the masses? Who or what, then, is the Antichrist? The answer is obvious: the historicized Jesus of the churches and the doctrines of blind faith, Self-sacrifice, obedience and the fetishization of weakness and poverty.

See BLACK SUN, ESCHATON and FRIEDRICH NIETZSCHE.

ANTIMATTER - Material composed of antiparticles that correspond to particles of ordinary matter, with the same mass but having opposite charge. Particles and antiparticles annihilate each other when brought together, releasing high-energy photons in the form of gamma radiation. This reaction has practical applications in medical imaging and antimatter has also been proposed as a fuel source (and potential weapon), though it is currently astronomically costly to produce.

ANNIE ANXIETY - Also known as Little Annie, Annie Bandez and various admixtures of these names. After performing with a backing band (the Asexuals) at New York's notorious Max's Kansas City restaurant in her teens (late 1970's e.v.), Bandez/Anxiety went on to work with Crass and many other groups spanning a variety of underground genres. Such variety is indicative of her style, which ranges from torch and cabaret to experimental to reggae and hip-hop and back to jazz. She also paints and acts and her memoirs are titled *You Can't Sing The Blues While Drinking Milk*.

AQUA REGIA - A mixture of one part nitric acid and three parts hydrochloric acid. Named as it is ("Royal Water") for its ability to dissolve the noble metals gold and platinum.

See GOLD.

ART OF NOISES - An approach to music deriving from a manifesto (*L'arte dei Rumori*) of the Futurist art movement, written by Luigi Russolo in the form of a letter to composer Balilla Pratella.

In this letter, Russolo traces the history of music and "noise" from the near silence of the world in ancient times. Once music was invented, it was necessary for musicians to create ever more complex and novel forms in order to stimulate the senses and emotions; thus gradually approximating the "noise-sound" which fully came into being in the ambiance of industrial cities. Russolo urged musicians to explore cities with "ears more sensitive than eyes" to find these Futurist noise-sounds and to organize them into new music.

For the purposes of the Futurist orchestra, essential noises could be grouped into six families:

1. Rumbles, Roars, Explosions, Crashes, Splashes, Booms

2. Whistles, Hisses, Snorts

3. Whispers, Murmurs, Mumbles, Grumbles, Gurgles

4. Screeches, Creaks, Rumbles, Buzzes, Crackles, Scrapes

5. Noises obtained by percussion on metal, wood, skin, stone, terracotta, etc.

6. Voices of animals and men: Shouts, Screams, Groans, Shrieks, Howls, Laughs, Wheezes, Sobs

See FUTURISM, INDUSTRIAL CULTURE, ALAIN PRESENCER and Z'EV.

ASTRAL · The Astral Plane and our corresponding astral bodies are a long-standing staple of occult lore. The Astral is described as a "higher" or more subtle plane of existence but yet close enough to our material world that it can be accessed through dreams. The skillful are said to be able to separate their astral body, made of more shadowy material, from the physical body and use it as a vehicle to travel the Astral Plane at will.

Indeed, a clue to the extreme age of this idea and its related practices is that the word "astral" means "starry" or "of the stars", from the Greek *astron* for star. Greek philosophers such as Plato and Aristotle held that the stars were made of a subtler, spiritual form of matter and that the human mind or soul was also made of the same kind of matter.

Even further back, shamanic cultures often contain stories of how a shaman might travel to the stars and learn from celestial teachers. Yu the Great, in the land that became China, even left diagrams of dance steps or paces for traversing the Celestial Ladder and the stars of the

Northern Bushel (our Ursa Major or Big Dipper).

See DREAMS, REMOTE VIEWING, SCRYING and SHAMANISM.

AVATAR · The term *avatar* derives from the Sanskrit for "descent" and refers to the deliberate appearance or manifestation of a deity in the physical world. Hindu legends tell of gods such as Shiva or Vishnu appearing in many various forms at different times.

See Æ, ANTICHRIST and RALPH CHUBB.

B

BANGKOK · The capital of Thailand and its most populous city, but more properly known as *Krung Thep* to the locals. Its royal Grand Palace and Buddhist temples stand amid notorious red-light districts and vibrant street life, humming with electricity and ghosts.

CLIVE BARKER · Liverpudlian author, artist, playwright and film director. Barker is perhaps best known for his *Books of Blood* anthologies and *The Hellbound Heart*, with the latter being the origin of the *Hellraiser* series of films. Several of the short stories from the *Books of Blood* have also been turned into films and Barker, himself, directed *Nightbreed* (based on "Cabal") and *The Lord of Illusions* (based on "The Last Illusion"), as well as the first *Hellraiser* film.

While Barker wrote quite explicit horror stories in his youth, his later works have taken a more broadly fantastical turn, which is reflected in his painting. Or vice-versa, in that his recent *Books of Abarat* series began as a series of 300 paintings before he even began writing.

Which highlights the fact that Barker is a truly fantastic artist, in both senses of the word.

BASENJI · A breed of hunting dog, classified as a hound, originating in central Africa. Notable for its unusual, yodel-like vocalization and for perhaps being the most ancient dog breed extant in the world today.

BASSENTHWAITE - Small village in Cumbria, England, at the foot of Skiddaw mountain and roughly a mile from Bassenthwaite Lake. According to the census of 2001 e.v., Bassenthwaite had a population of 412.

See BLACKBIRD and HAWTHORN.

HAKIM BEY - Pen-name of Peter Lamborn Wilson. Where Wilson has most notably written works on heretical Islam, Bey writes on various themes related to his idea of Ontological Anarchism. These ideas are best communicated by quotes from Bey, himself.

Ontological Anarchy is rooted in the metaphysics of Chaos. For Bey, Chaos is much like the *Dao* of Laozi and he says:

"CHAOS NEVER DIED. Primordial uncarved block, sole worshipful monster, inert & spontaneous, more ultraviolet than any mythology (like the shadows before Babylon), the original undifferentiated oneness-of-being still radiates serene as the black pennants of Assassins, random & perpetually intoxicated." (Chaos)

Bey's anarchism then progresses from an ontological realization (or remembrance) of this state of affairs:

"Everything in nature is perfectly real including consciousness, there's absolutely nothing to worry about. Not only have the chains of the Law been broken, they never existed; demons never guarded the stars, the Empire never got started, Eros never grew a beard.

"No, listen, what happened was this: they lied to you, sold you ideas of good & evil, gave you distrust of your body & shame for your prophethood of chaos, invented words of disgust for your molecular love, mesmerized you with inattention, bored you with civilization &

all its usurious emotions.

"There is no becoming, no revolution, no struggle, no path; already you're the monarch of your own skin--your inviolable freedom waits to be completed only by the love of other monarchs: a politics of dream, urgent as the blueness of sky." (Chaos)

That being said, the primary tactic for realizing Ontological Anarchy is the Temporary Autonomous Zone (TAZ). This is a vast and deep subject but we can define the TAZ rather simply. The Autonomous Zone is a space, large or small, where (to use of one of Bey's favored phrases) "the chains of the law have been broken". Bey explains how and where such spaces may exist:

"The 'map' is a political abstract grid, a gigantic con enforced by the carrot/stick conditioning of the 'Expert' State, until for most of us the map becomes the territory--no longer 'Turtle Island,' but 'the USA.' And yet because the map is an abstraction it cannot cover Earth with 1:1 accuracy. Within the fractal complexities of actual geography the map can see only dimensional grids. Hidden enfolded immensities escape the measuring rod. The map is not accurate; the map cannot be accurate [...] We are looking for 'spaces' (geographic, social, cultural, imaginal) with potential to flower as autonomous zones--and we are looking for times in which these spaces are relatively open, either through neglect on the part of the State or because they have somehow escaped notice by the mapmakers, or for whatever reason. Psychotopology is the art of dowsing for potential TAZs." (The Psychotopology of Everyday Life)

Which does then invite the need for a variety of strategies, tactics, methods and technologies for finding, creating and using such spaces. This may in itself be considered an artform, perhaps the most radical of our time.

See CHAOS and PSYCHOGEOGRAPHY.

BINAURAL BEATS · When two tones of slightly differing frequencies are run through stereo headphones into the two ears of a listener, there is an auditory illusion in which the tones seem to split the difference and merge into a single (third) low-frequency pulsation. This process can even trick the brain into perceiving frequencies that it really should not and these can be used to cause brainwaves to synch with the frequency (entrainment) and produce altered states of consciousness.

See BRAIN-MIND MACHINE and SIDEREAL SOUND.

THE BIRTHDAY PARTY - Influential gothic rock band from Australia, active between 1978 and 1983 e.v. Also once did a split 12" EP, *Drunk on the Pope's Blood/The Agony Is the Ecstasy*, with Lydia Lunch. Singer Nick Cave and guitarist Mick Harvey went on to form another legendary group, Nick Cave and the Bad Seeds.

BISM - In the Narnia stories of C. S. Lewis, Bism is the nation of the Gnomes. It is located 6,000 feet below Underland in the world of Narnia and is also known (understandably) as the Really Deep Realm. In addition to the Gnomes, the great lava rivers of Bism are also inhabited by Dragons and Salamanders. In this realm, gold and gems grow like fruits and are harvested by the Gnomes for food and drink. So used, their remains then take on the hardened, fossilized forms known by Men.

BLACKBIRD - Any of various birds the male of which is almost entirely black, such as the purple grackle, cowbird, red-winged blackbird or common English thrush.

See BASSENTHWAITE and HAWTHORN.

BLACK HUMOR - Humor that makes light of otherwise serious, frightening or disturbing subject matter by expressing irreverence or cynicism with regard to such subjects. The more specific form known as "gallows humor" explicitly shows how black humor can also express courage in the face of death or hopeless situations.

BLACK SUN · Variations on the image of a Black Sun have been proliferating through the fringes of culture at a gradually exponential rate over several decades. This appears to be a spontaneous process but what does this potent image signify? We can go back through history for some clues.

In antiquity, we find two Black Sun prototypes: the Egyptian Khephra and Roman Mithras. Khephra is the Sun at Midnight in the form of a scarab beetle, deep in the Underworld as the mirror of its noontime, overhead position. Conversely, Mithraic scholar David Ulansey convincingly argues for the Roman Mithras being a personification of a Platonic, Hypercosmic Sun (Sol Invictus) existing in a divine, "intelligible" realm beyond the "cave" of this universe.

Later, in European alchemy, the Black Sun (like the Death's Head) is a symbol of the *nigredo* or "blackening" phase associated with putrefaction and decomposition, a Saturnian anti-Sun. Likewise, bypassing lead, we might see feces as an inversion of gold, making the anus a sort of anti-Sun as well. Of course, this connects with the image of Khephra as a dung beetle.

In the more recent context of the growing mythology of "Nazi Occultism", we might consider the memes relating to the Vril Society that supposedly explored the ideas in Edward Bulwer-Lytton's novel *The Coming Race*. The novel concerns the discovery of a subterranean, telepathic "master race" called the *Vril-ya*, whose culture is powered by a mysterious energy called Vril. Vril energy can be directed both by technology and directly by the Vril-ya themselves through mental discipline. As this mythology has evolved among esoteric theorists and occult practitioners, it has been asserted that the source of the Vril is either an interior sun (echoes of Khephra) or some source deep in space or even beyond this dimension (echoes of the Hypercosmic Sun). Of course, the Swastika, itself, may be seen as a form of Black Sun.

The Black Sun may also find an analogue within the Cthulhu Mythos of writer H.P. Lovecraft in the form of the Daemon-Sultan Azathoth. Despite that humanoid-sounding title, Azathoth is described as "that amorphous blight of nethermost confusion which blasphemes and bubbles at the center of all infinity" and whose place is simultaneously "beyond time and space" and "outside the ordered universe" (like the Hypercosmic Sun of Mithraism).

Indeed, Lovecraft's colleague Clark Ashton Smith even uses the term in his story "The Devotee of Evil":

"...I do not think that the power is personal, in the sense of what we know as personality. A Satan? No. What I conceive is a sort of dark vibration, the radiation of a black sun, of a center of a malignant eons - a radiation that can penetrate like any other ray - and perhaps more deeply.

"For a long time past, my life-work has been to ascertain its true nature, and to trace it to its fountain-head. I am sure that somewhere in space there is a center from which all evil emanates."

The relationship between Azathoth and another of Lovecraft's deities, Yog-Sothoth (who is Time and All-Things-Together), is comparable to that of Hadit and Nuit in the Thelemic system of Aleister Crowley. Indeed, Azathoth's place at both the center of all infinity and yet beyond the ordered universe is reminiscent of Crowley's references to a circle whose center is everywhere and circumference nowhere found.

While Lovecraft and Smith were writing fiction (as Bulwer-Lytton was in *The Coming Race*), their ideas have been adopted by practicing Magicians such as those in the Esoteric Order of Dagon. Which brings us to explicit use of the Black Sun as a symbol for Chaos, generally, in the form of a black circle with eight radiant arrows as promoted by the Illuminates of Thanateros.

Of course, the Black Sun manifests most commonly during a solar eclipse, where sun and moon are conjoined - with all of the alchemical and psychological implications symbolically inherent in such an event.

As an archetype, the truth of the Black Sun probably both underlies, transcends and enfolds all of these facets, which merely reflect some aspect of that truth as projected though the lenses of the minds of men. What strange Dawn its (re)emergence heralds still remains unknown, except to perhaps a very few.

See ALCHEMY, CHAOSPHERE, HARRY CROSBY, ESOTERIC ORDER OF DAGON, ILLUMINATES OF THANATEROS, MAGNETIC NORTH, SODOMY and SURREALISM.

WILLIAM BLAKE - English painter and poet straddling the 18th and 19th centuries e.v. who developed a complex personal mythology around the sacred principle of poetic genius, which he equated with the Spirit of Prophecy.

Blake was an independent thinker in all major areas of life. He was opposed to slavery and believed in the equality of the sexes. His views on love and sexuality foreshadowed the later "free love" movement and polyamory. In the area of religion, Blake held to much Biblical imagery and the image of Christ as the intersection of God and Man but was also influenced by the mystical writings of Jakob Böhme and Emmanuel Swedenborg as well as his own visions.

Blake was little regarded in his own time but is now considered one of the greatest British artists.

See ANGEL and ESCHATON.

ANGELA BOWIE - Originally Mary Angela Barnett, Angela (or Angie) is a model and actress that was married to musician David Bowie over the 1970s e.v. and with whom she has a son, film director Duncan Jones. She also purchased the rights to produce a television series based on the Black Widow and Daredevil characters from Marvel comics · unfortunately about four decades too early.

BRAIN-MIND MACHINE · An apparatus of goggles and headphones used to induce relaxation and altered states of consciousness by way of coordinated rhythmic sounds and flashing lights to alter the brainwaves of the user. Also known as mind machines or light and sound (l/s) machines.

See BINAURAL BEATS and BRION GYSIN.

BROCCOLI · Edible, green plant known for its large, tree-like, flowering head. Broccoli is actually the same species (*Brassica oleracea*) as cauliflower, Brussels sprouts, cabbage and kale, which are all cultivars of wild cabbage. It is an excellent source of vitamin C and dietary fiber, as well as containing many other nutrients and immune-supporting and anti-carcinogenic compounds. Because these compounds are diminished by boiling, methods of cooking such as steaming, stir-frying and even microwaving are recommended, though it may certainly be eaten raw.

TREVOR BROWN · English artist based in Japan and popular for his "baby art" style, which combines figures similar to the "big eyes" paintings of Margaret Keane with fetishistic and paraphilia elements and aspects of Japanese popular culture (though perhaps we repeat ourselves).

See FETISHISM.

BULLROARER · A wooden slat attached to the end of a string or thong, forming an instrument that produces a roaring sound when whirled around one's head. Found all over the world and dating from paleolithic times. Variously used for ceremonial purposes, communicating over long distances or as a toy. Also known as a rhombos, turndun, thunder-spell, groaning stick or wind wand.

See DIDGERIDOO.

WILLIAM S. BURROUGHS · William Seward Burroughs was born into a prominent family in St. Louis, Missouri. His grandfather, also named William Seward Burroughs, had invented an adding machine and founded the Burroughs Adding Machine Company (later, the Burroughs Corporation). His maternal uncle was a publicist for the Rockefeller family. As things turned out, however, young William was meant for a very different sort of life than his family could have ever imagined.

For one thing, Burroughs was homosexual, which made him an outsider from the start and he later became one of the first authors to write explicitly on the subject. There were other things, though, that helped to put him on his unusual path: childhood visions of "gray monkeys", a nanny that taught him to call toads in the manner of old-time witches and early drug experiences with chloral hydrate at a boys' school in New Mexico.

We can talk about Burroughs as a writer or even as a Magician but we should begin by seeing him as an EXPLORER. He was an early student of a variety of "twilight sciences" that later became more well-known and/or controversial. He studied the General Semantics of Alfred Korzybski. He went to South America in search of *ayahuasca* or *yage* and its supposed telepathic properties two decades before Terence McKenna and long before the current fad. His use of one of Wilhelm Reich's orgone cabinets is described in Kerouac's *On the Road*. Burroughs was also a student of Scientology long before it was associated with Hollywood celebrities and was primarily an interest of intellectual, engineering types. Despite having criticisms of the organization, many Scientological ideas became essential themes of his worldview and writing.

And, of course, Magic. Burroughs' tastes in this area tended to run toward the primitive: fetishes, curses and sympathetic magic in general - though he later developed modernized operations along these lines using sound recordings, photographs, film and writing. He was also drawn to the psychedelic sorcery of Carlos Castaneda and the ancient Mesopotamian demons of the Simon *Necronomicon*. At the end of his life, Burroughs became an initiate of the Illuminates of Thanateros.

We would also do well to look at Burroughs' career in stages. The first of these is connected to his role in the Beat movement or phenomenon. Having a romanticized view of the criminal life and an allowance from his wealthy family, Burroughs was able to carve out a slightly seedy, urban niche for himself and was a personal influence on the younger Jack Kerouac and Allen Ginsberg. His first two novels, with the relatively self-explanatory titles *Junkie* and *Queer*, are fictionalizations of his life during this period. His breakthrough work, of course, was *Naked Lunch*, which is notable for its graphic and non-linear style.

However, where things really start to get interesting is with the so-called Nova (or Cut-Up) Trilogy: *The Soft Machine*, *The Ticket That Exploded* and *Nova Express*. These works all employ the cut-up method, where text is cut up and randomly recombined to create new text. Burroughs felt that this method allowed him to destroy the programming structures of reality and reveal hidden meaning. Broadly speaking, *The Soft Machine* deals generally with sexuality and biology, *The Ticket That Exploded* deals with control structures and *Nova Express* describes a conflict between destructive, hyperdimensional entities and those who oppose them.

Following the Nova Trilogy, there is a brief interlude that we might call the Academy 23 stage. Burroughs' idea for Academy 23 was a sort of network of groups and facilities for taking various ideas and technologies that he had encountered as an explorer and applying them to the kinds of issues brought up in the Nova Trilogy. In works such as *The Job*, *The Adding Machine* and *The Electronic Revolution*, these ideas and interests are synthesized and brought forward from his fiction and into practical discussion.

This leads to the final stage of Burroughs' writing career (the end of his life being largely given over to painting) in the Red Night Trilogy. While being a return to fiction, these works represent a marriage of the Nova mythology with the clearer vision and methodologies described in the Academy 23 works. These books are *Cities of the Red Night*, *The Place of Dead Roads* and his last major work, *The Western Lands*.

In terms of Burroughs' own mythology and aims, *The Western Lands* might be considered his masterpiece. Its plot concerns the search for a map to the Western Lands, the afterlife realm of the ancient Egyptians. The underlying theme is Death and how to beat it, something that would have been on Burroughs' mind at the end of his life as well being the last barrier to cross (as a human).

But it is even bigger than that. In *The Western Lands*, Burroughs puts forth a basic conflict: the One-God Universe (OGU) vs. the Magical Universe (MU). The OGU is static and entropic, while the MU is polycentric and dynamic. Both the Western Lands and the Magical Universe represent what Burroughs more abstractedly referred to as SPACE. All out of Time and all into SPACE. He considered this a matter of survival, an evolutionary imperative. For Burroughs, moving into SPACE did not just mean astronauts and space colonization - though it definitely DID mean that - but also something more that the Western Lands and the Magical Universe were descriptive of. As he says in the book:

"[O]ur policy is SPACE... anything that favors or enhances space programs, space exploration, simulation of space conditions, exploration of inner space, expanding awareness, we will support. Anything going in the other direction we will extirpate. The espionage world now has a new frontier."

See DMT, DREAMS, CUT-UP TECHNIQUE, ELECTRONIC VOICE PHENOMENA, FOUND RECORDINGS, BRION GYSIN, HARMALINE, ILLUMINATES OF THANATEROS, INDUSTRIAL CULTURE, TRANSGRESSIVE ART and VIRUS.

KATE BUSH · English singer, musician, songwriter, record producer and Commander of the Most Excellent Order of the British Empire (CBE). Her music has included both classical and ethnic elements and instruments with those of rock and pop in a unique personal style.

BUTTHOLE SURFERS · Texas rock band with absurdist and dadaesque qualities · particularly in their early live shows, which included films of car crashes and genital surgery, dancing mutants, fire, extreme cacophony and general mayhem.

C

DONALD CAMMELL · Scottish artist and filmmaker. At one pole of the entertainment industry, Cammell worked with U2, while at the other, he played the role of Osiris in Kenneth Anger's *Lucifer Rising* and is known for having written and co-directed the cult film *Performance*.

Cammell's father was a poet and knew Aleister Crowley, who lived near the family for a time, making the Great Beast a part of young Donald's childhood. In his teens, Cammell illustrated an edition of the story of King Arthur and later also painted society portraits.

Donald Cammell committed suicide in 1995 e.v. after his film *Wild Side* was cut by the producer. The collaborative novel *Fan-Tan*, which tells a tale of piracy in the South China seas, was written with actor Marlon Brando and published in 2005 e.v. after both Cammell and Brando's deaths.

See PERFORMANCE, NICOLAS ROEG and THELEMA.

CAPTAIN BEEFHEART · Stage name of American musician Don Van Vliet, whose style combined blues, rock and psychedelia with the completely experimental. Like *The Velvet Underground & Nico* album before it, Beefheart's *Trout Mask Replica* is very often referenced by later alternative musicians as a significant inspiration.

See DADA and SURREALISM.

CATASTROPHE THEORY · Originating in the work of French mathematician Rene Thom, Catastrophe Theory is part of the study of dynamical systems. As the name suggests, it describes how sudden and dramatic changes can result from much smaller changes in the equilibrium of nonlinear systems.

See CHAOS and TERENCE MCKENNA.

CEFALU · Coastal city in Sicily, named *Cephaloedis* or *Cephaloidion* (meaning "headland") by the Greeks and later Latinized as *Cephaloedium*. In modern times, Cefalu is a major tourist destination.

A farm house in Cefalu served as Aleister Crowley's "Abbey of Thelema" between 1920 and 1923 e.v. The Abbey was inspired by the anti-monastery of the same name described in Rabelais' *The Life of Gargantua and of Pantagruel*, where the only rule was "Do What Thou Wilt," and was devoted to the observance and practice of Crowley's own philosophical and magical system.

Filmmaker Kenneth Anger spent a summer at the Abbey several decades later, uncovering Crowley's elaborate wall murals that had been whitewashed when the Thelemites were expelled by Mussolini's government. Anger's film of these murals, *Thelema Abbey* (1955), is regrettably lost. This is doubly unfortunate as the building itself has been allowed to fall into nearly complete ruin, though it still remains something of a place of pilgrimage.

See THELEMA.

CHAOS · The word "Chaos" is of Greek origin with a core meaning of "gaping" or "wide open", thus referring in cosmology to an empty void or abyss in the beginning of things. This concept is set in opposition to "Cosmos" and its meanings of order and arrangement or even ornament, thus the created world.

But the matter is actually much more complicated than that.

The ancient Greek Chaos described by Hesiod is interpreted more as a vast ocean of moving, formless mass than as mere emptiness, with the created world emerging from that mass. This is comparable to the primordial Chaos couple Tiamat and Abzu of Babylonian mythology as personifications of salt and fresh water, whose matings produced the younger gods, and with the later formation of the world from the body of Tiamat.

After millennia of static and enforced social hierarchies, law-based religions and eventual clockwork notions of natural order, Chaos is now associated with discord, disruption and existential vertigo. This is an important aspect of Chaos to be sure and has held an archetypal presence within the ancient Roman festival of Saturnalia and the medieval European Christmas traditions of the Lord of Misrule or Abbot of Unreason. Our contemporary Discordians, Antinomians, Chaos Magicians and all would-be tricksters, pranksters, blasphemers, heretics and iconoclasts serve this aspect of Chaos.

But this is only one aspect of Chaos and a somewhat outer and reactive one, as well. Again, there is much more to it.

To shift perspective, Chaos Theory in mathematics studies phenomena that may seem random or chaotic in the colloquial sense but are in fact totally deterministic. These phenomena simply involve systems that are incredibly complex and dynamic from the ordinary human perspective. This is the world of the notorious "butterfly effect" where the flapping of a butterfly's wings may set atmospheric forces in motion that affect the path of a hurricane or tornado on the other side of the planet.

On the other hand, the physicist Werner Heisenberg invoked "potentia" as a subatomic realm metaphysically underlying actuality and John Wheeler spoke of "quantum foam" as the turbulent foundation of the universe - both of which are evocative of ancient cosmological ideas of Chaos.

Also, in such sciences as biology and economics, there is the concept of Spontaneous Order - a term which implies the reconciliation of Chaos and Cosmos. Spontaneous Order is the novel state or pattern that emerges from the free interaction of elements within a system. Spontaneous Order as a process allows for evolution through variation, competition, feedback and adaptation. It is dynamic and tends to overflow with abundance as many new and unexpected innovations emerge from its rich complexity. Examples of Spontaneous Order include ecosystems, the evolution of language, free economic markets and neural networks.

Synthesizing all of these ideas, we can perceive a Chaos that is ALL. Abyss and Ornament. Oceanic, foamy *potentia* and deeper, deterministic (but malleable and dynamic!) order. Disturbing and smoothing, like water - the old symbol of Chaos.

While others merely play with - or are played with by - its most superficial trappings, the true Magician approaches this Chaos as his greatest love and seeks to know it, shape it and be shaped by it ever more deeply.

See HAKIM BEY, CATASTROPHE THEORY, CHAOSPHERE, ILLUMINATES OF THANATEROS and TIAMAT.

CHAOSPHERE - In the fiction of Michael Moorcock, there is a symbol that is representative of Chaos. It has eight arrows radiating outward from a central source. This stands in opposition to the symbol for Law that is just one arrow. Many paths or directions against just the one. This symbol was adopted in the early days of the Chaos Magic(k) movement and became more of a Black Sun symbol, with the eight arrows radiating from a solid black circle. This is often referred to as the Chaosphere.

The term applies more specifically, however, to a tool described in Peter J. Carroll's book *Liber Null*. There, the Chaosphere is described as a three-dimensional version of the symbol. It may be hollow and one of the arrows may be removed for use as a magical weapon, features that facilitate a wide variety of operations. Carroll does also say that it may take other forms altogether.

The key issue is that it is the Chaoist equivalent of the traditional Magical Lamp. It is activated with a combination of paradox and life force, whereby it becomes "a purposely created crack in the fabric of reality through which the stuff of Chaos enters our dimension". Carroll also suggests that the creation and placement of such devices at key locations around the world might facilitate and accelerate radical changes to being, culture and reality.

See BLACK SUN, CHAOS, ESCHATON and ILLUMINATES OF THANATEROS.

RALPH CHUBB - English poet, artist and printer. Strongly influenced by William Blake, Chubb came to identify himself as Ra-el-phaos (or Raf), the guardian angel of Albion, and developed a personal mythology rooted in childhood stories, the tropes of his own sexuality and in reaction to the horrors of the First World War.

Ra-el-phaos was the avatar of the Holy Spirit in the form of a young boy, "naked perfect and unblemished", come to initiate a new age upon the Earth. The aesthetic theme of idealized male youth thus seems to pervade Chubb's work as an expression of not just his amorous desire but also of a desire for purity, as it is supported by fairy tale imagery of knights and elves and paradaisal, utopian innocence, garnished with astrological, numerological and other occult symbolism.

See AVATAR, WILLIAM BLAKE and EPHEBOPHELIA.

CODEX - In law, a code or volume of statutes. More generally, a manuscript or volume of scripture or classic text.

LEONARD COHEN - Canadian singer, songwriter, musician and author. While more widely know for his musical career, Cohen actually spent his early years as a writer, publishing novels and books of poetry. It is thus not surprising that his songs have a very literary quality as they deal with themes of love, sex, depression, religion and politics.

COIL · From Latin *colligere* by way of Old French *coillir*, meaning to gather together, particularly in a winding form · hence the coils of a snake, of rope or of wire. Alternatively, to move in a winding course. Separately, from Old French *acueil*, meaning collision, a commotion or turmoil. To boil or seethe.

ITHELL COLQUHOUN · British occultist and painter born in India. Rejected for membership by the Hermetic Order of the Golden Dawn, she later joined the Typhonian version of the Ordo Templi Orientis (OTO). Expelled from the London Surrealist Group, she developed such Surrealist techniques as graphomania (drawings deriving from flaws in paper) and parsemage (using paper to skim charcoal or chalk dust off the surface of water). Colquhoun also produced a body of occult writings, including a biography of the Golden Dawn's Samuel Liddell "MacGregor" Mathers called *The Sword of Wisdom*.

See QABALA and SURREALISM.

DENNIS COOPER · American author, poet and performance artist especially notable for his *George Miles Cycle* of novels, dealing with themes of sex, violence, drug use and teenaged existentialism.

COPAL · A resin produced from various tropical trees, used in making varnishes and ink. However, the name comes from Classical Nahuatl *copalli*, referring to incense, for which copal has been used by both ancient and contemporary Mesoamerican peoples. It is also used as a solar incense (alternative to frankincense) in ceremonial magic. Usually yellow or amber in color, though sometimes white, it does also come in black.

See BLACK SUN.

HARRY CROSBY · American poet and publisher of the so-called "Lost Generation" era that came of age during World War I. Crosby came from a prominent banking family and was related to J.P. Morgan, Jr. by marriage.

Crosby's career as Crosby may be said to have truly begun when he began sleeping with an older, married woman named Mary (or Polly, later Caresse) Peabody. This led to scandal and divorce; after which, their open affair became an open marriage and generally hedonistic lifestyle devoted to travel, drug use, sexual affairs and the arts underwritten by Crosby's trust fund.

In 1927, Harry and Caresse founded Black Sun Press and published works by Hart Crane, T.S. Eliot, Ernest Hemingway, James Joyce, D.H. Lawrence and Ezra Pound in addition to Crosby's own books of poetry such as *Red Skeletons*.

Crosby's work involved a fixation on solar imagery, the sun being a symbol to him of perfection, enthusiasm, freedom, heat, and destruction. He had a sun tattoed on the sole of his foot (and a cross on the other) and signed his name with a black solar doodle at the end. In this signature, the ending "y" curves up into an arrow pointing at the sun and giving it a secondary and inverted quality as receptive orifice. Of course, as mentioned, the business was also Black Sun Press.

Long-obsessed with death and suicide, Harry Crosby killed himself with a bullet to the head at the age of 31. His body was found with that of one his lovers, who had either killed herself earlier or been murdered by Crosby. Caresse kept Black Sun Press going into the 1950s e.v.

See BLACK SUN and SURREALISM.

CUT-UP TECHNIQUE · Tristan Tzara created a method for producing poetry by randomly pulling written words from a hat. Later, the painter Brion Gysin discovered a variation of the method after rearranging strips of cut newspaper that he had placed underneath to protect a tabletop while he cut paper with a razor blade. He passed the method to William S. Burroughs, who really ran with it.

As Burroughs explains it:

"The method is simple. Here is one way to do it. Take a page. Like this page. Now cut down the middle and cross the middle. You have four sections: 1 2 3 4 ... one two three four. Now rearrange the sections placing section four with section one and section two with section three. And you have a new page. Sometimes it says much the same thing. Sometimes something quite different--(cutting up political speeches is an interesting exercise)--in any case you will find that it says something and something quite definite."

Burroughs considered the results to be divinatory, saying that the future leaks out when you cut through the present. Burroughs and Gysin also applied the technique to audio tape, as have many others since. It has been widely applied to video and even to habits and the randomization of behavior.

See WILLIAM S. BURROUGHS, BRION GYSIN, INDUSTRIAL CULTURE, LIMINALITY and SURREALISM.

D

DADA - Dada began as an informal art movement - anti-art, really - in reaction to the horrors of the First World War and the new phenomenon of international, mechanized slaughter that it introduced. Dada was in turn a form of destruction aimed at aesthetics, reason, logic and sense - all things that might be considered hypocrisy in the postwar world. Dada was about blasphemy, iconoclasm, nihilism, chaos and absolute protest against everything. It was a universal NO.

But destruction clears space where new creation comes rushing in. When torn up paper is allowed to fall randomly upon a background and is presented as a collage, this is a nihilistic - even hostile - statement about aesthetics and artistry within the context of Dada. However, such random processes later found a home within the Surrealist movement, where the same collage might be interpreted as an irruption of the unexpected, a communication of alien novelty and an alchemical fixing of the volatile.

Indeed, the Dadaists developed several techniques later gainfully employed by the Surrealists, such as assemblage, collage and photomontage. Dada may also be considered an ancestor of Situationism, Fluxus, culture jamming and even "joke" religions such as Discordianism and the Church of the Subgenius.

See BOYD RICE and SURREALISM.

SALVADOR DALI · Spanish painter and the Surrealist most well-known by the general public, though he was despised by Andre Breton. Both relationships stem from Dali's megalomaniacal eccentricity and his commerciality; for which, Breton called him "Avida Dollars" in an anagram of his name. Politics was another area of conflict, though, as Breton sought to make Surrealism politically Communist and Dali considered himself an Anarcho-Monarchist (as well as an aesthetic Roman Catholic).

In his best-known works, Dali paints in the style of the Old Masters, as he insisted that one must learn to do. However, these works also depict dreamlike scenes and often include illusory double images. The effect of these double images is greatly enhanced by the clarity of the technical style. Such works are rooted in Dali's own Paranoiac-Critical Method, for which there is a separate entry in this book.

Dali also worked to a lesser extent in architecture, fashion, photography and even film collaborations with Luis Buñuel (*Un Chien Andalou, L'Age d'Or*), Alfred Hitchcock (*Spellbound*) and Walt Disney (*Destino*).

See ONAN, PARANOIAC-CRITICAL METHOD, SCATOLOGY and SURREALISM.

DARKNESS · The opposite of Brightness. Darkness wanes and waxes in complement to the presence of Light. Even within the presence of Light, however, there are still dark objects. Such objects are dark because they absorb photons rather than reflecting them. This also follows a spectrum or scale in that a black object is darker (absorbs more photons) than a blue object, which is darker than a yellow object. For that matter, a single color such as blue or yellow can itself also be lighter or darker and the darkness of black can be seen as the end of a grey spectrum whose other end is white. These gradations of light and darkness are referred to as "value" in art and design.

Metaphysical Darkness is the Unmanifest and the Unknown, the place beyond the campfire light of conscious understanding or even perception, Individual or societal. This Darkness is receptive and ever opens up before us, to Infinity. It is Mystery and can thus justifiably inspire both wonder and fear.

Scotobiology is the study of the biological effects of Darkness. An example of such effects is the human body's need for darkness to produce melatonin and regulate the immune system.

The love and fear of Darkness are called *nyctophilia* and *nyctophobia*, respectively, for the ancient Greek goddess Nyx, personification of Night.

See DARK-SKY MOVEMENT and UNKNOWNS.

DARK-SKY MOVEMENT · A campaign to preserve the night sky by reducing light pollution for the purposes of increasing the number of stars visible at night and to reduce the negative effects of excess light on living organisms, particularly those that are nocturnal. Means include the establishment of dark-sky oases or preserves in rural or wilderness areas and the use of special lighting fixtures that reduce skyglow in urban areas.

DEATH · As an event, the termination of life, when all biological functions necessary to the continuation of a living organism have ceased. As a name, Death may also refer to the personification of this process · the "Grim Reaper" · as a generic version of such dignitaries as the Hindu Yama, Greek Thanatos, Roman Mors, Abrahamic Azrael or the Santa Muerte of contemporary Mexican folk religion.

Obviously, Death weighs heavily on the human mind as it is the end of Being or at least of the familiar mode of Being. On the one hand, it is clothed in all forms of ending, decay, inevitability and fate, of which it is the Ultimate. On the other hand, for many, it is clothed in ideas of radical transformation, otherworldly realms of spirit, reincarnation, reward and punishment. And, of course, Mystery. Confounding and inspiring, Death stalks the landscapes of Art, Magic and Religion.

Science, too. Medically defining the precise moment of death is problematic because the definition of life remains slippery. Patients are being rescuscitated after longer and longer periods of clinical death. The movement for radical life extension seeks to push the boundaries of life both conceptually and technologically until death is crowded out of existence entirely.

However, even if with some strange aeon, Death, itself, should die, the unfaced issues that surround it and our psycho-spiritual reactions to them may yet remain with us as Death's ghost.

See ANGEL, HORSEMEN OF THE APOCALYPSE, JACKAL, VULTURE and YEW.

DECALCOMANIA - Technique for generating images by applying paint to a piece of paper that is then either folded to create a mirrored pattern and/or pressed against another sheet or surface. The resulting image can then be elaborated upon.

See MAX ERNST and SURREALISM.

SIR JOHN DEE - English mathematician, astronomer, astrologer and sometime tutor and advisor to Queen Elizabeth I. Dee was also a great innovator as a Magician and created several new magical systems in service to his greater vision.

The intelligentsia of Dee's time were aflame with a sense of apocalyptic vision much like the New Age and New Aeon ideas prevalent today. The angels with whom Dee communicated charged him with the restoration of the true faith and the re-establishment of divine order upon the Earth. In addition to his work in England, Dee went on a crusade throughout Europe communicating his vision to other intellectuals of the time and heads of state such as King Stefan of Poland and the alchemically-minded Holy Roman Emperor Rudolf II.

The magical systems developed by Dee and his partner Edward Kelley (about whom there is a separate entry in this book) were generally created through a process of prayer and scrying. Following what we would today call invocations and statements of intent, Kelley would gaze into a "shew stone" (crystal or black mirror) and report what he saw to Dee. This resulted in the reception of some complex methodologies for further work. The spirits or angels seen by Kelley even instructed the pair in their own language, Angelic or Enochian, with the latter being the common name today and perhaps the most well-known feature of the systems.

The system in Dee's *De Heptarchia Mystica* concerns the ministering hierarchy of the planetary angels. His elemental Watchtowers concern those of Spirit, Fire, Air, Water and Earth and sub-elements, while the Aethyric system describes thirty planes of existence representing the shades of gray between the highest spiritual realm and the material world. The Watchtower and Aethyr systems merge in *Liber Scientae, Auxilii, et Victoriae Terrestris* (The Book of Knowledge, of Might, and of Terrestrial Victory), where the Governors of the Aethyrs are held to rule specific lands or parts of the world.

Amidst all of this, it is important to remember that Dee was also perhaps the most scientifically learned man of his day, had the ear of the Queen and collaborated heavily in the fields of cartography and navigation while advocating trade and national strength. He was one of the first - if not *the* first - to use the term "British Empire" and thus essentially set the wheels in motion for its manifestation from concept to global reality. In this sense, though dying poor and out of favor under a new ruling House, John Dee might be considered the most successful Magician in history.

The character of Prospero in William Shakespeare's play *The Tempest* is said to be based on Dee - which would mean that *Forbidden Planet*'s Doctor Morbius is, as well. Perhaps most strangely, fictional spy James Bond is also based to an extent upon Dee. The code name 007 was used by Dee in his correspondence with Queen Elizabeth. The 00s represent eyes and the 7 refers to the *Heptarchia*. The manner in which Dee wrote the 007 will be familiar to Master Masons (and fans of Rudyard Kipling). This trivia was passed to Bond's creator Ian Fleming by Aleister Crowley and the rest is film franchise history.

See ANGEL, ESCHATON, HIEROGLYPHIC MONAD, SIR EDWARD KELLEY, SCRYING and THELEMA.

DEEP LISTENING · Practice developed by composer Pauline Oliveros. Deep Listening may be thought of as active rather than passive listening. It means intentionally going into music, ambient sounds or even your own thoughts, imagination and dreams with full attention and continual alertness, which Oliveros also calls Sonic Awareness.

SAMUEL R. DELANY · American author and literary critic notable for his science fiction works dealing with themes of perception and memory, sexuality, language and mythology.

DERANGEMENT · "A poet makes himself a visionary through a long, boundless, and systematized disorganization of all the senses. All forms of love, of suffering, of madness; he searches himself, he exhausts within himself all poisons, and preserves their quintessences. Unspeakable torment, where he will need the greatest faith, a superhuman strength, where he becomes among all men the great invalid, the great criminal, the great accursed · and the Supreme Scientist! For he attains the unknown! Because he has cultivated his soul, already rich, more than anyone! He attains the unknown, and if, demented, he finally loses the understanding of his visions, he will at least have seen them! So what if he is destroyed in his ecstatic flight through things unheard of, unnameable: other horrible workers will come; they will begin at the horizons where the first one has fallen!" · Arthur Rimbaud

DESERT ROSE · A succulent shrub (*Adenium obesum*) native to Africa and Arabia, with white tubular flowers that turn red or pink as the flower flares into five petals. The sap is used as a fish toxin and arrow poison throughout much of Africa. The term "desert rose" also applies, though, to rosette formations of gypsum or baryte crystals containing abundant inclusions of sand grains.

DIDGERIDOO · A wind instrument made from a long tube (usually wood or bamboo) that is blown into to create a low drone.

See BULLROARER and DRONE.

DMT · *N,N*-Dimethyltryptamine, a powerful hallucinogen. Structurally related to serotonin and melatonin, the brain processes it quite quickly and its effects last for less than half an hour. That is when smoked or injected in a pure form. However, when taken orally as in the traditional Amazonian ayahuasca brew, the effects last much longer but are less intense. To be effective orally, DMT must be combined with a monoamine oxidase inhibitor such as harmaline. The structurally related drug 5-MeO-DMT is also sometimes referred to simply as DMT and is even more potent.

See WILLIAM S. BURROUGHS, HARMALINE, TERENCE MCKENNA and ALEXANDER SHULGIN.

DOCTRINE OF SIGNATURES · An aspect of herbalism and early medicine in which it was believed that the features of plants might indicate what maladies they could treat. For example, the red extract of bloodroot would be used to treat the blood. This idea that "like cures like" is very similar to the idea of Sympathetic Magic and surely derived from it. This is the imitative principle behind doll or fetish spells and simulatory rituals such as sprinkling water to cause rain. This doctrine is distinct (or maybe not) from John Locke's original conception of Semiotics (ideas are the signs of things and words are the signs of ideas) which is sometimes called the Doctrine (or Theory) of Signs.

See FETISHISM.

DOET (HECATE) · 2,5-Dimethoxy-4-ethylamphetamine, also called Hecate, is a phenethylamine and amphetamine drug created by Alexander Shulgin. It is particularly long-lasting, with trips running 14-20 hours. Currently appears to be quite obscure and what little information exists is somewhat contradictory. Shulgin described its use as a fairly calm experience with the potential for cognitive enhancement while other anecdotes describe very strange and even horrifying experiences.

See ALEXANDER SHULGIN.

DREAM · Dreams are sequences of images and other sensations with accompanying thoughts and emotions that occur in the mind during certain stages of sleep. They are much like the experiences of waking life but can be much more strange, though even the strangest may seem perfectly ordinary during the experience. Dreams are usually involuntary but may be controlled in what is called Lucid Dreaming.

Some ancient cultures believed that dreams were actual travel experiences of the spirit or soul (or an aspect of it). The gods or the dead might visit one in a dream or the future might be foretold. Some still believe these or similar things. In some Daoist and Sufi sects, initiatory lineages might even be passed in dream experiences.

In psychology, there are several schools of thought about dreams and their meanings or significance but they are widely considered to reveal information about the deeper levels of the mind (as well as processing information from the day).

Whether considered psychologically or magically, dreams were of great importance to Surrealism in that they formed a complement to the experience of waking life and were a half of the Super-Reality of which both were divided parts.

See ASTRAL, WILLIAM S. BURROUGHS, ESOTERIC ORDER OF DAGON, HOWARD PHILLIPS LOVECRAFT, SHAMANISM, SLEEP and SURREALISM.

DRONE · A musical note or chord that is continuous through most or all of a piece. Drone is also the name of a minimalist type of music that is specifically based on such sounds.

See DIDGERIDOO, HURDY GURDY, KARLHEINZ STOCKHAUSEN, VELVET UNDERGROUND and LA MONTE YOUNG.

E

ELECTRONIC VOICE PHENOMENA · Electronic Voice Phenomena (EVP) describes the unexplained appearance of human-sounding voices appearing in electronic media, most usually ambient recordings. In fact, the voices are often not heard at the time of such recordings and only appear later during playback. Such voices often claim or appear to be spirits of the dead.

Thomas Edison worked on a machine for communicating with the dead in the 1920s e.v. but EVP really came into its own with the work of Konstantin Raudive four decades later. Working with a variety of electronics experts and under strict conditions, Raudive recorded over 100,000 tapes and the results of his work were published in English as the book *Breakthrough* in 1971 e.v.

See DEATH and FOUND RECORDINGS.

ENERGY · In purely physical terms, energy is the ability of force to produce effects over distance. In Aristotelian philosophy, *energeia* is the activity that bridges the gap between potentiality and actuality. Within ourselves, we may talk of energy in terms of our physical or mental vitality, either metaphorically or in the sense of an actual life force. This latter is very relevant to magical practice as the advent of science led to a shift from the earlier spirit-based model of Magic to an energy-based one. Here, Magic is effected by means of combining image and energy that is usually amplified by emotion or sexual arousal. However, pre-scientific and even cultures under the spirit-based model still usually have some concept of personal power such as *mana* (Polynesian) or *qi* (Chinese).

EPHEBOPHILIA - A primary sexual attraction to mid-to-late adolescents. While laws in many locations restrict legal adults from acting upon such attractions, ephebophilia is distinct from pedophilia (sexual attraction to pre-pubescent children) and is not generally considered abnormal in itself by psychologists.

See HAKIM BEY, WILLIAM S. BURROUGHS and RALPH CHUBB.

EQUINOX - The crossing of the equator by the sun, resulting in night and day being of equal length in all parts of the world. The vernal equinox marks the passage from winter to spring in the northern hemisphere and occurs around March 21st. The autumnal equinox marks the passage from summer to fall or autumn in the northern hemisphere and occurs around September 23rd. In the southern hemisphere, the equinoxes are reversed. The word "equinox" comes from Latin for "equal night".

See LIMINALITY, SOLSTICE and THELEMA.

ERGOT - A group of fungi within the genus *Claviceps* but notably *Claviceps purpurea*, which grows on ears of rye and related cereal plants and grasses. Humans and animals that consume ergot develop a poisoned condition known as ergotism but also more colorfully as "holy fire" or "St. Anthony's fire" after the monks of the Order of St. Anthony who specialized in its treatment. Symptoms of ergotism include mania and psychosis, convulsions and gangrene. Speculations have been made that less harmful amounts of ergot were used in ritual settings by ancient Greek and Germanic groups. The psychedelic drug lysergic acid diethylamide (LSD) was synthesized from ergotamine, an alkaloid produced by *Claviceps purpurea*.

See BLACK SUN and LSD.

MAX ERNST - German Dadaist and Surrealist. While opinions, tastes and criteria for judgment may vary widely, Max Ernst may be considered the Surrealist *par excellence*, especially with regard to the conscious integration of "occult" material into his work in service to the Surrealist ideal of the Super-Reality. Ernst drew explicitly from alchemical ideas and imagery and his lover Leonora Carrington depicted him as a shaman in her own work.

Ernst worked with a number of styles, media and techniques, but this alchemical approach is perhaps most perfectly exemplified by his collages. Indeed, he defined collage as the "alchemy of the visual image" and the French writer René Crevel called him the "wizard of barely perceptible disarrangements" for his work. Indeed, Ernst created entire graphic novels of his collages, such as *La femme 100 têtes* (*The Hundred-Headless Woman*, 1929 e.v.) and *Une semaine de bonté* (*A Week of Kindness*, 1934 e.v.). These masterpieces were created using illustrations from Victorian novels and encyclopedias.

Alchemy is also apparent in many of his paintings, notably landscapes such as *Men Shall Know Nothing of This* and *Marriage of Heaven and Earth* which can be said to depict the Super-Reality directly.

See ALCHEMY, DADA, DECALCOMANIA and SURREALISM.

ESCHATON - The furthest or last, referring in Christian theology to the "end times" and final state of the world. Eschatology, then, is the study of doctrines concerning such issues as prophetic events, judgment, death and resurrection and the promised Eternal Kingdom to follow. However, the term may also be applied to doctrines of the same type in other religions or even in secular futures studies.

An interesting and important concept that has been circulating through cultural currents relevant to this book is known as the Immanentization of the Eschaton. Put most simply, this means creating "Heaven (or whatever equivalent is preferred) on Earth" - the establishment of something like paradaisal afterlife conditions or the post-apocalyptic Kingdom in the experiential and material here and now. This term can be applied either sincerely or derisively to any utopian scheme. Magicians have taken up the idea and use the term to describe a general project for transforming reality in its entirety, extending various "New Aeon" concepts.

The primary concern with such aims is that it rather depends on what one's idea of "Heaven on Earth" would be like, something that surely differs widely from person to person. As with all living arrangements, then, the best Eschaton to Immanentize would be one with maximum personal autonomy and novelty with conditions of voluntary participation.

See ANTICHRIST, WILLIAM BLAKE, SIR JOHN DEE, ESOTERIC ORDER OF DAGON, ETERNITY, HOWARD PHILLIPS LOVECRAFT, ILLUMINATES OF THANATEROS, TERENCE MCKENNA and THELEMA.

ESOTERIC ORDER OF DAGON (EOD) - Cult group that took over the local Masonic hall in "The Shadow over Innsmouth" by H.P. Lovecraft and provided the name for a real-life occult group based on the serious magical exploration of concepts and methods described in Lovecraft's fiction. Despite the name, this group incorporated the aims and techniques of all such groups in Lovecraft's work, including the Starry Wisdom sect, Cthulhu cult and witch covens.

Like many other occult groups, the EOD proclaimed its own new era: the Aeon of Cthulhu Rising. Relevant areas of exploration included chaos, atavism, mutation, astronomy and astrology, higher mathematics and hyperdimensionality. Methodologies of exploration included dreaming, scrying, glossolalia, sexual magic(k), experimental drug use and the grounding of received visions through art, music and literature. Many in the EOD were also influenced by Aleister Crowley and Thelema, though more primitive sorceries were also highly favored in EOD rites.

See CHAOS, DREAMS, ESCHATON, FUTURISM, LIMINALITY, HOWARD PHILLIPS LOVECRAFT, SCRYING, SURREALISM, THELEMA and XENOPHILIA.

ETERNITY · Usually refers to the totality of infinite and linear Time, with the concept of the Eternal referring to anything of infinite duration within Time. However, Eternity also may refer to a manifold of existence that transcends linear Time and its mechanical determinism. In this sense, Eternity refers to a meta-infinity of Time beyond mere everlastingness and yet potentially present (or accessible) within each moment.

See ESCHATON.

EUREKA · A 1983 e.v. film directed by Nicolas Roeg. It tells the story of a Klondike prospector who finds an enormous amount of gold and becomes fabulously wealthy. Two decades later, he is living on an island and both fortune and island are being eyed by others · including his own daughter and her husband, who may also be contesting for his soul.

See NICOLAS ROEG.

F

FETISHISM · The term "fetish" applies to material objects believed to have inherent power and used for religious or magical purposes. Examples would include idols, dolls, bones and bags or bundles of plant, mineral and man-made items. However, there is also sexual fetishism, where desire or arousal can become attached to a secondary object. For example, something like women's undergarments or shoes somehow become representative of a woman as a whole in terms of being an object of attraction. This is distinct from paraphilias such as bondage or dominance and submission that are often termed fetishes, especially in connection with "fetish" clubs or events.

See EILEEN AGAR, DONATIEN ALPHONSE FRANCOIS DE SADE, SHAMANISM and SURREALISM.

DION FORTUNE · Pseudonym of Welsh occultist Violet Mary Firth, derived from her family motto *Deo, non Fortuna* (By God, not Fate). Fortune was a member of the Theosophical Society and participated in two off-shoots of the Hermetic Order of the Golden Dawn · the Alpha et Omega and Stella Matutina orders · before forming her own Fraternity (later, Society) of the Inner Light. In addition to her non-fiction writing · which included the classic *Psychic Self-Defense* · she also wrote magical stories and novels such as *Moon Magic* and *The Sea Priestess*.

See MOON and QABALA.

FOUND RECORDINGS · Random audio recordings taken from the ambient environment or haphazardly from media such as radio or television, or randomly found recordings made earlier by others (such as used cassette tapes).

See WILLIAM S. BURROUGHS and ELECTRONIC VOICE PHENOMENA.

FRACTAL · Infinitely complex, never-ending patterns created by repeating a simple process over and over in an ongoing feedback loop. Zooming out or zooming in to look at the fractal on different scales, the same pattern is repeated. This property is referred to as "self-similarity". Fractal patterns can be found throughout nature, such as in the branching nature of trees. The self-similarity of fractals can most easily be seen in computer-generated examples like the Menger Sponge or the well-known Mandelbrot set, named for mathematicians Karl Menger and Benoit Mandelbrot, respectively.

See CHAOS.

GAVIN FRIDAY · Founding member of Irish post-punk band The Virgin Prunes. He is also an accomplished painter.

See HONEYGUIDE.

FUTURISM · Primarily Italian art movement of the very early 20th century e.v. Futurism was a revolt against the perceived weight and stagnancy of Italy's romanticized past, the notion that the whole country was primarily a museum. The Futurists loved and promoted speed, violence, youth and electricity while adoring automobiles, aeroplanes and industry.

Because Futurism embraced every aspect of art and craft including architecture and even cooking, it did much to shape the spirit and aesthetics of the coming century. Unfortunately, like Surrealism later, it became associated with authoritarian political ideologies or it could have gone so much further. Today, philosophies such as Extropianism revive the spirit of Futurism and apply it to newer and even more transformational technological possibilities but sadly have not yet matched Futurism in the arts.

See ART OF NOISES, INDUSTRIAL CULTURE and MARS.

G

JOHN GIORNO · American poet and performance artist who organized the Dial-A-Poem service where recorded poems could be heard by telephone. Giorno also worked with Robert Moog to create "Electronic Sensory Poetry Environment" installations and happenings.

Giorno was at one time a friend and lover of Andy Warhol and maintains the old New York "bunker" residence of William S. Burroughs, which is in the building where Giorno has lived for decades.

See WILLIAM S. BURROUGHS and WARHOL SUPERSTARS.

GLITCH · Genre of music based on sounds of technical malfunction or failure such as distortion, hardware noise and software bugs. It would also be possible to use errors or glitches in the creation of music as departure points for new creations.

See ALCHEMY, INDUSTRIAL CULTURE, SURREALISM and UNKNOWNS.

GLOSSOLALIA · Incomprehensible speech in an imaginary (or imaginal) language, sometimes occurring in a trance state, an episode of religious ecstasy, schizophrenia or some admixture of these and comparable states.

See ESOTERIC ORDER OF DAGON, TERENCE MCKENNA and SHAMANISM.

GLOWWORM · Any of a number of wingless insects or insect larvae that give off a phosphorescent light; especially, the wingless female or the larva of the firefly (*Lampyridae*).

See MOONMILK and WAVEFORM.

GOLD · A heavy, yellow, metallic chemical element with a high degree of ductility and malleability. Its elemental symbol is Au (from its Latin name *aurum*) and its atomic number is 79. Apart from its traditional use as money and in jewelry, gold has important applications in technology and even medicine. While not the rarest or most costly, it is the archetypal precious metal and a symbol of perfection. This is because gold is very non-reactive and will not rust or tarnish and because it is also traditionally associated with the sun, as silver is with the moon.

See ALCHEMY, GOLDEN SECTION and SCATOLOGY.

GOLDEN SECTION · Another name for the Golden Ratio, also called the Divine Proportion, which is said to play a key role in the human perception of beauty. Two quantities are in this proportion if their ratio is the same as the ratio of their sum to the larger of the two quantities. It is found throughout nature and has applications in architecture, music, drawing and painting.

The Golden Section (*Section d'Or*) was also the name of an important exhibiting group organized by Cubist painter Jacques Villon, the brother of Marcel Duchamp.

See GOLD.

GOLDEN TRIANGLE · An area overlapping the point where the borders of Thailand, Laos and Burma meet, designated by the confluence of the Mekong and Ruak rivers. Noteworthy for being one of the world's highest-producing areas in the opium trade and the smuggling of other drugs.

See BANGKOK.

GRANULAR SYNTHESIS · The creation of new sound from microsamples of sound called "grains" for the formation of highly malleable soundscapes.

See ANALOGUE SYNTHESIS and MUSIQUE CONCRETE.

GREENSLEEVES · An English folk song known from the Elizabethan period. Sometimes thought to be about a prostitute or enthusiastic amateur · or a woman mistaken for such · due to contemporary associations of the color green, as in "The Old Green Gown" from the same era (think grass stains). However, one might also speculate upon the latter song as a play upon the former.

GREEN CHILDREN · There is an English legend about the appearance of two green children in the Suffolk village of Woolpit in late medieval times. A boy and a girl, they gradually adjusted to local life and lost their green color. The boy was sickly and eventually died. The girl, however, thrived and was said to be quite lusty. The children had originally spoken an unknown language but the girl eventually learned English and told of being from an underground realm called St. Martin's Land.

This legend plays an important part in Herbert Read's novel *The Green Child*, though the novel is an original and modern story.

BRION GYSIN · Canadian painter and author born in England but fairly international in heritage and life journey. At the tender age of 19, Gysin was briefly associated with the Surrealists but was expelled from the movement by Andre Breton at the start of his first exhibition. After serving in the Second World War, he wrote a book on slavery titled *To Master, a Long Goodnight.*

Gysin later moved to Morocco and opened a restaurant called The 1001 Nights in Tangiers. He hired the Master Musicians of Jajouka · who Timothy Leary called a 4,000 year old rock and roll band, and who were brought to international attention by Brian Jones · to perform on the premises. He also learned about local Magic, finding a curse charm in his restaurant demanding that he leave. He did, in fact, lose the business. However, Gysin also came to incorporate grids and asemic glyphs inspired by Moroccan sorcery into his own art.

Next big stop was the famous Beat Hotel in Paris (9 rue Gît-le-Coeur), where William S. Burroughs also lived, and the two enjoyed a lively collaboration. Gysin discovered the cut-up technique and passed it to Burroughs as described elsewhere in this book, and they wrote *The Third Mind* together. Many years later, when Burroughs began a golden years foray into the visual arts, he said that he had learned everything from Gysin and could never have painted while he was still alive.

Gysin also developed the Dreamachine, the first work of art meant to be viewed with the eyes closed. This was a spinning, stroboscopic tower that used the flicker effect to induce visions within the mind's eye of the viewer.

See BRAIN-MIND MACHINE, WILLIAM S. BURROUGHS and CUT-UP TECHNIQUE.

H

HARMALINE · Reversible monoamine oxidase inhibitor found in the seeds of Syrian rue (*Peganum harmala*) and the yage or ayahuasca vine (*Banisteriopsis caapi*). In the case of the latter, it is traditionally brewed with the leaves of the dimethyltryptamine-rich chacruna plant (*Psychotria viridis*) so as to render the DMT orally active in a shamanic visionary potion. Monoamine oxidase is something like a chemical immune system and the harmaline knocks it out so as to amplify the effects of the DMT. For that reason, the more commonly available Syrian rue seeds are also used with DMT-bearing plants to create ayahuasca analogues or may even be combined as a booster with other substances such as psilocybin mushrooms.

See WILLIAM S. BURROUGHS, DMT, TERENCE MCKENNA and PSILOCYBIN.

HAWTHORN · The Common Hawthorn (*Crataegus monogyna*) is a flowering shrub or small tree native to Europe, northwest Africa and western Asia. The "haws" or fruit of the Hawthorn are used in making jam and wine. Hawthorne was also traditionally known as "May" because the blossoming of its flowers was so strongly identified with that month. It was thus emblematic of May Day and witches were also said to make their brooms from it.

See BASSENTHWAITE and BLACKBIRD.

HIEROGLYPHIC MONAD · *Monas Hieroglyphica* is the name of both an esoteric symbol created by John Dee and a book that he wrote to explain its meaning and significance. Unfortunately, the text is rather difficult and is generally thought to merely be the notes for a greater (perhaps oral) teaching. The actual glyph is a specialized form of the symbol for Mercury that combines other planetary and elemental symbols and is representative of cosmic unity.

See ALCHEMY, SIR JOHN DEE, TERENCE MCKENNA and MERCURY.

TERRENCE HIGGINS TRUST · British charity dedicated to preventing the spread of the human immunodeficiency virus (HIV) and to promoting understanding of its impact. Founded by the friends of one of the first Individuals in the United Kingdom to die (1982 e.v.) from the HIV-caused Acquired Immunodeficiency Syndrome (AIDS).

See VIRUS.

HONEY · Thick, sweet food comprised mostly of fructose and glucose and made by bees from the nectar of flowers. Honey has been used as a food and medicine around the world and from very ancient times. Its medicinal use derives from antiseptic properties and it has also been widely used as a preservative because it does not spoil.

The sweet and preservative qualities of honey often lead to poetic, mythological or religious symbolism, such as in a "land of milk and honey" or in connoting immortality. Honey, water and other ingredients are used in the production of mead; a traditional beverage with its own mythological links, notably among Germanic peoples with regard to poetic inspiration.

HONEYGUIDE · Birds that leave eggs in the nests of other bird species where, upon hatching, the young honeyguides will then use their sharp beaks to puncture the eggs of the host birds or kill their chicks. Honeyguides feed on wax and grubs and at least one species will lead humans to bee hives so as to engage their help in this purpose. The name is derived from this behavior.

See GAVIN FRIDAY.

HORSEMEN OF THE APOCALYPSE · Personifications of Conquest (or Pestilence), War, Famine and Death described in Revelation 6:1-8 of the Bible.

See DEATH.

HURDY-GURDY · The hurdy-gurdy might be described as the platypus of musical instruments. It is a sort of violin with a keyboard and a crank. Its sound is something of a marriage between that of the violin that it somewhat resembles and the drone of bagpipes. Played by a master, its effects are truly mesmerizing.

See DRONE.

I

I CHING · The ancient Chinese "Classic (or Book) of Changes" is a collection of 64 patterns commonly known as hexagrams. Each of these hexagrams is a unique pattern of six lines which are either solid or broken and represent the *yang* and *yin* forces respectively. The I Ching is usually employed as a divination manual but may also be read as a cosmological treatise.

For divinatory purposes, the hexagrams are built up line by line either by tossing yarrow stalks or flipping coins. Once a hexagram has been received, its corresponding text can be looked up in the book for what insight it may provide.

Cosmologically, we might think of the I Ching and its hexagrams as being comparable to the Periodic Table of chemical elements · except that the hexagrams represent dynamic forces or conditions rather than fixed substances. These then map out the forces of change that exist in the cosmos.

The German mathemetician Gottfried Leibniz was impressed by the structure of the I Ching, Aleister Crowley called it the initiated system of Chinese Magic and psychologist Carl Jung employed it frequently as a means for exploring the unconscious through his idea of the synchronicity of inner and outer events. Composer John Cage used the I Ching to write music (see his *Music of Changes*) and science-fiction author Philip K. Dick used it to write his novel *The Man in the High*

Castle.

See TERENCE MCKENNA.

ILLUMINATES OF THANATEROS (IOT) · Influential occult group conceived in the 1970s e.v. that brought Chaos Magic(k) to the world, particularly through the publication of Peter J. Carroll's *Liber Null* and *Psychonaut* and Ray Sherwin's *The Book of Results*, though the IOT existed as a conceptual aegis for a decade before it became a real organization.

The name harkens back to the notorious Illuminati and combines the names of the Greek gods of Death and Sex, Thanatos and Eros (an alchemical *coniunctio* or union of opposites). Chaos Magic(k), itself, was originally something of a melange of ideas and practices derived from Aleister Crowley, Austin Spare, Daoism and Tantra.

When the IOT actually became a functioning membership organization, it was formally known as the Magical Pact of the Illuminates of Thanateros or simply as The Pact. As Peter J. Carroll described it in a historical essay titled "The Pact (IOT) · The Story So Far":

"The Pact has but two aims. Firstly the pursuit of the Great Work of Magic and pleasures and profits attendant to this Quest. Secondly to act as a Psychohistoric Force in the Battle for the Aeon."

In addition to the metaphysics of Chaos, itself, Chaos Magic(k) also became known for its eclecticism, which Carroll describes in the same essay as "whatever forms of Techno-Shamanism, Tantric Goetia or Greco-Egyptian Quantum Physics we can make work for us".

Unfortunately, as Chaos Magic(k) spread and became more popular, the eclecticism and fear of anything resembling dogma overshadowed the actual Chaos and this once radical approach became subject to the same softening, whitewashing and political correctness as Wicca before it and seemingly anything else that becomes too popular.

But Chaos will always be there for those who seek it.

See WILLIAM S. BURROUGHS, CHAOS, CHAOSPHERE, ESCHATON, AUSTIN OSMAN SPARE, THELEMA and ZOS KIA CULTUS.

INDUSTRIAL CULTURE - For our puposes here, the term "Industrial Culture" refers to the wider manifestations surrounding the Industrial music genre.

Foreshadowings or precursors of the Industrial aesthesis include Italian Futurism, Musique Concrete, Brutalist architecture, Andy Warhol's "Death and Disaster" painting series, the Space Age mythology and tape cut-ups of William S. Burroughs, the fiction of J.G. Ballard, electronic music in general but especially Lou Reed's *Metal Machine Music* album and the emergence of Kraftwerk. When the Industrial music scene emerged in the 1970s e.v., it drew from and often explicitly referenced all of these things and was known for taking more inspiration from philosophy, fine art and literature than from previous musical styles.

In the cradle of the genre proper, the Industrial Records label founded by the members of Throbbing Gristle, the term "Industrial" referred to the manner of constructing the music. This is like Warhol calling his studio The Factory. Later, however, groups such as Einstürzende Neubauten began using drills, jackhammers and other industrialized instumentation after the fashion suggested by the Futurist Art of Noises (though Boyd Rice had previously attached an electrical fan to a guitar).

Industrial music surprisingly merged with its opposite - Disco - in the 80s to produce the Industrial Dance genre associated with acts like Ministry, My Life with the Thrill Kill Kult, Front 242 and so on. Also at this time, the Cyberpunk genre of science fiction was foreshadowing the post-industrial Information Age, the internet and a different form of technological aesthetic, which was folded into the Industrial Dance culture and facilitated its explosion into a bewildering variety of subgenres in the 90s.

Much of the original Industrial aesthetic was conceived in a dystopian spirit and as something of a reaction to things that were celebrated by the Futurists. However, many of these attempts at a dystopian aesthetic were in actuality embraced by fans as beautiful and desirable. On the dancefloor level, so to speak, this lead to a milieu permeated with the vital and aggressive spirit of the original Futurists but with a darker aesthetic.

See ANALOGUE SYNTHESIS, ART OF NOISES, WILLIAM S. BURROUGHS, CUT-UP TECHNIQUE, FUTURISM, KRAUTROCK, LSD, MUSIQUE CONCRETE, HERMANN NITSCH, BOYD RICE, VELVET UNDERGROUND and Z'EV.

ISOLATIONISM · Lifestyle stance based on varying degrees of cultural, aesthetic and social detachment and introversion balanced with Self-cultivation. Isolationism could be said to be a spectrum of positions running from complete asociality and hermitage to someone who simply opts out of following the "news" and spectacle of popular culture while preferring to give their attention to their own interests and the company of like-minded intimates.

The term also became applied to an ill-defined sub-genre of "colder" or "darker" ambient music ranging along a similar spectrum, with themes or moods of alienation and withdrawal or merely of solitude and introspection.

J

JACKAL · Family of small, carnivorous canines native primarily to Africa and the Middle East but also to West and South Asia. Like the coyote · which is sometimes referred to as the American jackal · it is also a proficient scavenger. The Golden Jackal native to North Africa, however, is now recognized as a subspecies of grey wolf.

Which brings to mind the jackal-headed, ancient Egyptian god Anubis (more properly, Anpu). Because jackals are scavengers, they are known to dig up graves and devour corpses. So, Anubis or Anpu transforms this role and is set as the protector of graves and tombs and even as the embalmer of the dead and guide of souls. In her novel *Her-Bak: The Living Face of Ancient Egypt*, Isha Schwaller de Lubicz has one of her characters hold forth on the essential or *neter* quality of the jackal. So it is explained:

"[H]e cleans the highways. The jackal's function is digestion, transforming putrid flesh into life-giving nourishment; what for other beings would be infectious poison, in him becomes an element of life, after the destructive element has been transformed."

When Anubis or Anpu weighs the Heart of the deceased against the feather of Truth (Maat), he judges and divides the corruptible and the incorruptible, one from the other.

See DEATH and VULTURE.

JANUS · Roman god of beginnings and endings, doors and gates, passages, thresholds and transitions. Janus appears with two faces, on the front and back of his head, looking forward and behind, and carries a key in his right hand. The month of January is named for him.

See LIMINALITY.

DEREK JARMAN · British stage director, filmmaker and artist notable for such films as *Jubilee* (in which Queen Elizabeth I and John Dee are transported to the punk-dominated Britain of 1977 e.v.), *The Angelic Conversation* (combining dreamlike, homoerotic imagery with the sonnets of Shakespeare) and *Blue* (which combines a spoken narrative concerning Jarman's work against a continuous blue screen) as well as creating music videos for the Sex Pistols, Marianne Faithfull, Throbbing Gristle, Marc Almond, The Smiths, the Pet Shop Boys and more.

See ANGELS, SIR JOHN DEE and OSTIA.

ALFRED JARRY · French Symbolist author primarily known for the play *Ubu Roi* and the creation of 'Pataphysics.

Ubu Roi tells the tale of how Pere Ubu, a character from Jarry's previous play *César-Antéchrist*, goes on an aburdist, over-the-top rampage, leading a revolution, killing the king of Poland and generally tyrannizing the populace. Elements of the play are borrowed from Shakespeare's *Macbeth*, *Hamlet* and *King Lear*. Jarry also wrote several more Ubu plays that were not performed in his lifetime.

'Pataphysics is the study of what lies beyond metaphysics (which, itself, means "beyond physics"). It is the science of imaginary solutions, unusually extended metaphors, puns, exceptions and incompatibles.

See SURREALISM.

K

SIR EDWARD KELLEY · Also known as Edward Talbot, Kelley acted as the medium and scryer in the magical operations of John Dee. This work was described earlier in the entry on Dee, so the focus here will be on Kelley's own nature and activities.

Kelley had a book and a quantity of red powder that he claims to have been led to finding by some sort of spiritual creature. With this powder and the secrets of the book, he claimed to be able to create a tincture that transmuted base metals into gold. Legends tell that Kelley even demonstrated this.

However, Kelley was known to be a bit of a scoundrel. Prior to his association with Dee, it is said that his ears had been cropped as punishment for some crime. Furthermore, Kelley was later imprisoned and Dee died in poverty. This would suggest that they did not possess the secret to making gold, no matter what may have been "demonstrated" on isolated occasions.

This highlights the magical work, though. For any who study it, it surely stands out as being beyond the stuff of a mere scam from Kelley as scryer.

See ALCHEMY, ANGEL, SIR JOHN DEE and SCRYING.

KETAMINE · Dissociative anesthetic used in human and veterinary medicine. Research has shown it to be effective in treating depression, addiction and epilepsy. Ketamine also produces a variety of effects such as delirium and hallucination depending upon dosage, leading to recreational use where ketamine may be thought of as comparable to dextromethorphan (DXM) or phencyclidine (PCP). In higher dosages, ketamine use is characterised by a sense of detachment from the physical body and the external world.

Ketamine was used extensively by neuroscientist and psychonaut John C. Lilly, who favored its use in his work because he found that its effects were much more predictable by dose than with other compounds such as LSD or psilocybin.

YVES KLEIN · French artist known for developing a color of paint known as International Klein Blue that is so vivid and intense that it is said to have a disturbing effect upon some people. Klein would take objects such as a reproduction of a famous statue or even a world globe and appropriate them as his own art by painting them his special blue color. He is shown in the film *Mondo Cane* creating a work by using the bodies of nude models for applying the paint.

KRAUTROCK · Term originating in the English press for a genre of music emerging in Germany (particularly Dusseldorf) around 1970 e.v. and combining psychedelic and progressive rock with electronics. Early Krautrock musicians came from jazz and experimental classical backgrounds, which also strongly influenced the basic style and sound. Groups such as Kluster (or Cluster), Can and Neu! typify this style while groups like Kraftwerk and Tangerine Dream pushed the use of synthesizers into more mechanical and minimalist styles, respectively. Krautrock was in turn an influence on the later development of Industrial and Post-Punk.

See ANALOGUE SYNTHESIS, INDUSTRIAL CULTURE and KARLHEINZ STOCKHAUSEN.

KUNDALINI - A force or energy held to reside at the base of the spine, with differing theories as to both its nature and proper arousal. First described in the Upanishads, the term can mean both bowl- or pot-like and ringed or coiled. The latter leads to Kundalini often being imaged as a snake and described as a "serpent force", though this could also be taken in the more abstract sense of a potential yet to be unfurled. Much, much, much later, the Kundalini is further personified as a goddess, specifically an aspect of Durga.

Methods for the awakening of Kundalini and the guiding of its force up the spine generally take the form of either active training of the mind, body and control of vital energies (things such as concentration, meditation and breath and muscle exercises) or in the removal of blocks that may prevent spontaneous and natural arousal (through the breaking of social and personal conditioning, cultivating quietness of mind and even temporary, direct empowerment by another practitioner). As in so many things, a balance of the two approaches is probably best.

The Kundalini has psychosexual connotations that reconcile the use of the term *libido* by both Sigmund Freud (sexual energy) and Carl Jung (psychic energy).

It is interesting to consider here the *kundabuffer* organ described by Georges Gurdjieff in his *Beelzebub's Tales to His Grandson*. The kundabuffer, in the story, is an organ implanted by angels into early humans to help them endure the stresses of a catastrophe. It is later removed but too late - its presence has left a permanent imprint upon the beingness of Man. It caused people to mistake the transitory for the eternal and thus to perceive reality backwards. One interpretation of this residual imprint is what we might refer to as the false personality or character as distinct from the Self. This distorting buffer can certainly divide us from not only our own life force but the energies of the world.

With that being said, we can perhaps even further stress the combination of the two methods or paths described above for both contacting these energies and remanifesting them in new and more desirable forms.

See ENERGY and SODOMY.

L

GEORGES LAKHOVSKY · Russian inventor of the Multiple Wave Oscillator (MWO), a machine controversially presented as a treatment for diseases such as cancer. In use, the patient sits between two radiating antennas in the form of concentric rings designed according to the golden ratio, where he or she is bombarded with the full spectrum of energy frequencies. The theory is that each cell of the body will oscillate in resonance with its own frequency and that the body as a whole will then be energetically reset as it should be (diseases being energetic disharmonies). All of this aside, the MWO has also been used to induce altered states of consciousness and visionary experiences, sometimes in conjunction with psychotropic drugs.

See ENERGY, GOLDEN SECTION and LSD.

PHILIP LAMANTIA · American Surrealist poet who published his first book, *Erotic Poems*, at the age of 19. Participated in peyote rituals with the Washo tribe of Nevada.

See SURREALISM.

LIMINALITY · Inbetweenness. Relative to any intermediate state, phase, condition, time or location. Twilight bridges day and night.

Bridges cross lands over bodies of water. The shore is where the land meets the sea. Hypnagogic and hypnopompic states cross the threshold of waking and sleeping. A literal threshold divides inside from outside. Adolescence comes between childhood and adulthood. The old, extended Christmas festival transitions from the old year into the new.

The liminal is indeterminate and uncertain, liquid and unshaped, full of possibility.

Ritual creates liminality on demand. In an initiation, one or more participants may be taken out of the context of their former selves and lives, reduced to a more fluid and malleable state and then reformed with a new sense of Self and new role. This applies to either a tribal warrior's initiation or to a school graduation ceremony. In an overtly magical ritual, the same process is applied to the very conditions of reality either in part or whole.

See CHAOS, CUT-UP TECHNIQUE, EQUINOX, ESOTERIC ORDER OF DAGON, JANUS, PARANOIAC-CRITICAL METHOD, SHAMANISM, SIDEREAL SOUND, SOLSTICE, SUBLIMINAL, SURREALISM, UNKNOWNS and ZOS KIA CULTUS.

LONDON · Greater London is a ceremonial county and administrative district of southeastern England, consisting of the ancient City of London and 32 metropolitan burroughs. It is the capital of both the country of England and the United Kingdom of Great Britain and Northern Ireland.

Greater London is large enough to contain over four New Yorks and is presently home to around 8.3 million residents. The actual City of London, though, is quite small · only roughly a square mile in size. This area is famous for being home to the trading and financial services industries. The gross domestic product of London, alone, is greater than that of Belgium or Sweden. In Collin de Plancy's *Dictionnaire Infernal*, Mammon is said to be Hell's ambassador to Great Britain.

London is approximately 2,000 years old. Much of the city was destroyed in the Great Fire of 1666 e.v. but only six people were killed. Since that time, however, London ruled for centuries as the cultural crossroads of the world and has untold layers of complex social and environmental history intricately folded within itself.

See LOST RIVERS OF LONDON.

LOST RIVERS OF LONDON · London's main river, the Thames, is widely known. However, numerous tributaries of both the Thames and the river Lea that used to flow openly through the city have been lost or submerged within the folds of London's historical layers. The largest of these is the Fleet, which gives its name to Fleet Street. It is now a sewer, as are a number of the lost rivers. Another, the Walbrook, was the site of the original Roman settlement. In recent years, plans have been set in motion to recover some of these lost waterways.

See LONDON.

FEDERICO GARCIA LORCA · Spanish poet, playwright and friend of Salvador Dali. Lorca is said to have been shot by Nationalist militia members for his known Republican sympathies and ties in the Spanish Civil War. His ethos regarding his vocations was that "[t]he artist, and particularly the poet, is always an anarchist in the best sense of the word. He must heed only the call that arises within him from three strong voices: the voice of death, with all its foreboding, the voice of love and the voice of art."

See SALVADOR DALI.

HOWARD PHILLIPS LOVECRAFT · American writer of pulp fiction stories with fantasy, horror, occult and science fiction elements for magazines such as *Weird Tales* during the period between the First and Second World Wars.

The thing about Lovecraft is that he made the weird tales *really* weird. He created an entire mythology of incalculably ancient and unimaginably alien monster-gods, the forbidden tomes of their lore and the unspeakable rites for propitiating and summoning them. All of this became even more real for readers when he shared his mythology with his friends and colleagues such as Clark Ashton Smith, Robert Bloch, Frank Belknap Long and August Derleth and allowed them to add to it.

Lovecraft wove his tales against backdrops of infinite cosmic time and space that make Man look like a microbe, and around hyperspatial dimensions and irregular geometries that are incomprehensible to most today but were even moreso back then. His stories regularly deal with themes of chaos or atavism and the possibilities for transmogrification or at least madness that can result from exposure to either. All of these tropes and themes are more familiar to us today thanks to Lovecraft's diffuse legacy but they were a powerful psychic shock at the time.

For this reason, Lovecraft drew some attention from the Surrealist movement and could even be said to have been an informal Surrealist, himself. He would have rejected this label outright, as it clashed with both his rationalist and materialist attitude and very traditional personal aesthetic tastes. However, his work is right in line with Surrealist interests, including the frequent references to the importance of dreams in several stories and the very fact that some of Lovecraft's ideas came directly from his own dreams.

For similar reasons, Lovecraft's works have also drawn the attention of occultists and Magicians - which, again, would have mortified Lovecraft, as his more purely literary fans never tire of pointing out. However, it completely misses the point to tell a Magician that something is "not real" as making What-is-Not become What-Is forms the basic premise of Magic.

Lovecraft was apparently quite pagan in his youth and this repressed impulse, combined with his conscious scientific interests and deep fear of Otherness can be easily seen as the subconscious stew from which his pantheon of Azathoth, Yog-Sothoth, Nyarlathotep, Shub-Niggurath, Cthulhu and so on were born via his dreams and stories.

In the world of Chaos Magic, especially, where Reality is whatever you can get away with, Lovecraft's mythology is perfectly suited to the Magic of a new, cosmic and transhuman age.

See CHAOS, DREAMS, ESCHATON, ESOTERIC ORDER OF DAGON and SURREALISM.

LSD - Lysergic acid diethylamide, commonly known as "acid". The effects of LSD include alterations of mood, thinking process and time-sense, visual distortions, synesthesia and even spiritual experiences. According to Timothy Leary, reactions to LSD experiences generally depend upon three elements: set, setting and dose. Set refers to mindset or psychological state while setting refers to social and environmental factors.

Originally synthesized from ergot fungus as a possible respiratory and circulatory stimulant by an employee of Switzerland's Sandoz Laboratories named Albert Hoffmann. After accidentally absorbing some of the drug through his skin, Hoffmann discovered its extremely powerful psychoactive effects during his later bicycle ride home. This occurred on April 19, 1943 e.v. and later came to be celebrated as Bicycle Day, especially on its 50th anniversary.

In the 50s, LSD was used experimentally by psychiatrists for the purpose of unblocking repressed subconscious material. Legendary actor Cary Grant is known to have undergone such therapy. During this time, LSD was also experimented with by the US Central Intelligence Agency as part of the MKULTRA mind control program and for chemical warfare applications.

LSD is most commonly associated, though, with the psychedelic youth culture that emerged a decade later. Through the arts, the creative potential of the drug eventually had transformative effects on popular media. However, it is worth noting that LSD also played a significant role in the Industrial music culture of the 80s in support of aesthetics that were quite the opposite of those Flower Power days. Despite what some might claim, particular values and aesthetics do not seem to emerge from the psychedelic experience, itself.

What this suggests is that Chaos is big and caters to many tastes.

See ERGOT, INDUSTRIAL CULTURE and SYNESTHESIA.

M

ANGUS MACLISE · Original drummer for the Velvet Underground, having particpated in La Monte Young's Theater of Eternal Music with John Cale. Maclise had an interest in Aleister Crowley and thought to make a film of Crowley's *Diary of a Drug Fiend*. He was also interested in Tibetan mysticism and did make the soundtrack for one of the all-time classic psychedelic films, Ira Cohen's *The Invasion of Thunderbolt Pagoda*. Maclise made proto-Industrial music from tape cut-ups, drones, spoken words and electronics. He died in Kathmandu in 1979 e.v. from pulmonary tuberculosis and this experimental music from the 1960s and 70s was only released around the turn of the new century.

See DRONE, LA MONTE YOUNG, THELEMA and VELVET UNDERGROUND.

MAGNETIC NORTH · The Earth has a magnetic field that envelops the whole planet and magnetic fields have north and south poles. The poles of the Earth's magnetic field are separate locations from the geographic poles of the Earth as a (rough) sphere and move over time due to magnetic changes in the planet's core. However, the magnetic poles are near to the geographic poles.

According to a lost work known as the *Inventio Fortunata*, there is an island or mountain at either the North or Magnetic North Pole called the Rupes Nigra (Black Rocks). The Rupes Nigra is supposed to be composed of magnetic rock or lodestone, which is why all compass needles point toward it. It is said to be found in the midst of a whirlpool fed by the indrawing of four seas, dividing four other islands that surround it.

So it was described by the famous map-maker Mercator to John Dee. As a result, the Rupes Nigra not only appeared on maps during the 16th and 17th centuries but its description may have influenced Dee's conception of the four Elemental Watchtowers in his magical systems. Moreover, some of the later lore of the Black Sun in its relation to the Vril energy and hollow-earth theories sounds reminiscent of the Rupes Nigra, which might also be viewed as a terrestrial counterpart to the Pole Star.

See BLACK SUN, SIR JOHN DEE, ENERGY and SNOW.

MARIMBA - A musical instrument somewhat like a xylophone, consisting of a series of hard wooden bars, usually with resonators beneath, played by being struck with small hammers.

See MARC ALMOND.

MARS - The fourth planet from the Sun in our solar system is named Mars for the Roman god of Spring and War. Mars rules both astrologically and magically over energy, vitality, enthusiasm, impulse, drive, libido, war and surgery. Its traditional metal is iron.

See FUTURISM.

ROBERTO MATTA - Chilean painter associated with Surrealism and Abstract Expressionism. Created a non-euclidean Tarot with Leonora Carrington and Charles Duits.

See SURREALISM.

ROSE MCDOWALL · Angel-voiced singer, musician and witch from Scotland who first came to attention with Jill Bryson as the duo Strawberry Switchblade. After this popular success in the 1980s e.v., she has since been a regular collaborator with a number of interconnected groups such as Death in June, Current 93 and Nurse with Wound. McDowall also did a number of 60s and 70s covers with Boyd Rice under the group name Spell.

See BOYD RICE and STEVEN STAPLETON.

TERENCE MCKENNA · American author of *Food of the Gods* and other works. McKenna also wrote two important books with his brother Dennis: *The Invisible Landscape* and *Psilocybin: Magic Mushroom Grower's Guide* (where the brothers used the pseudonyms O.T. Oss and O.N. Oeric).

The roots of McKenna's vision lie in both a 1971 e.v. quest to La Chorrera, Columbia in search ayahuasca and in the mathematics of the I Ching. This vision was presented to the world in *The Invisible Landscape* in 1975. By the 1990s, McKenna was being called the Timothy Leary of the Rave Culture.

Key to McKenna's vision was the use of psychedelic drugs, particularly the tryptamine compounds active in ayahuasca and psilocybin mushrooms (he was less enthusiastic about purely synthetic or so-called "designer" drugs). On the one hand, he viewed the substances as scientific instruments, akin to a microscope or telescope but with the focus on the psyche and the nature of reality. On the other, he also viewed these things shamanically and affirmed that they were teachers. Indeed, one of the things for which McKenna is most known is his descriptions of hyperspatial alien entities · "self-transforming machine elves" · contacted by smoking pure DMT.

He advocated "heroic" (large) doses of these substances so as to really break through into the experience but he also advised much reflective thought and thorough integration of the experiences. Both of these suggestions are in the true shamanic spirit and contrary to the habits of mere recreational thrill-seeking. McKenna's position was that these compounds had played a significant role in our early evolution as humans and could and would play a similar role in a comparable forward leap now.

The other side of McKenna's vision was concerned with Time and Novelty. In studying the patterns of the I Ching (as described elsewhere in this book) and the time-keeping system of the possibly psilocybin-influenced Mayan calendar, McKenna became convinced of an inherent pattern of increasing Novelty within the structure of Time.

Novelty is the new or original - the creative - contrasted with repetition and entropy. McKenna saw Novelty increasing throughout human history. Moreover, the *rate* of increase was also increasing. He called this the Timewave and predicted a singularity of infinite Novelty would be reached on December 21, 2012 e.v. In this, McKenna was also strongly influenced by the philosophy of Alfred North Whitehead and the idea of *concrescence*, the coming together of processes into the formation of a substance or entity (in this case, a concrescence of Novelty).

The cause of the Timewave, McKenna speculated, was an object in the future that was so infinitely novel and disruptive of reality that it acted as an attractor, drawing all of history toward itself. He referred to this transcendental object as the *Autopoietic Lapis* or "Self-created Stone" - consciously using the word "Stone" in the alchemical sense. He thought that this object might be some sort of time machine because of the causality-disrupting nature of such technology. The purpose of working with psychedelics was to tune into this singularity so as to prepare for it (hence the mushroom growing guide). Of course, in the spirit of disrupting causality, the project might also be seen as something of a self-fulfilling (autopoietic) prophecy.

McKenna's predictions about 2012 gradually became a fairly

well-known cultural meme. However, two unfortunate incidents occurred in the meanwhile. First, McKenna died of brain cancer in 2000. Then, his personal books and papers were destroyed in a fire in 2007. The 2012 meme was left to itself as a cultural phenomenon and degenerated into just another generic End-of-the-World scenario.

Now, 2012 has come and gone. McKenna seems to have been wrong. Can his vision be rehabilitated under these circumstances? While he spoke in some of the cliches common to the post-World War II "Baby Boomer" generation, McKenna was firmly rooted in Shamanism and Alchemy, which are perennial and archetypal patterns of human thought. He was aware of John Dee's previous, similar, heavenly campaign and consciously referenced it in his own. If nothing else, the 2012 meme would have been expressed very differently if McKenna had lived to preside over it.

We might say that the vision is certainly philosophically valid and inspiring but that, like so many, McKenna made his mistake on picking a date. The sky did not fill with UFO time machines on the morning of December 21, 2012 as he suggested it might. However, many truly miraculous social and technological events are occurring today with the potential for truly profound ontological and eschatological change. We might do well to keep in mind the words of cyberpunk author William Gibson: The future is already here - it is just not fully distributed yet.

So, perhaps we did reach a singularity of some kind in 2012 and simply have not fully caught up to it as a whole culture or species. Or, at the very least, perhaps the Autopoietic Lapis is still there, not at the end of history but in an ever-accessible Eternity, waiting for us to manifest it.

See ALCHEMY, SIR JOHN DEE, DMT, ESCHATON, ETERNITY, GLOSSOLALIA, HARMALINE, HIEROGLYPHIC MONAD, I CHING and PSILOCYBIN.

MDMA - "Ecstasy" or 3,4-methylenedioxy-methamphetamine, a drug with euphoriant and entactogenic effects. Originally used experimentally for psychotherapeutic purposes in the 1970s e.v., Ecstasy became a very popular recreational drug through the Acid House and rave cultures of the 80s and 90s. It is often used in combination with other drugs such as LSD, psilocybin mushrooms or ketamine.

See AMPHETAMINES, KETAMINE, LSD, PSILOCYBIN and ALEXANDER SHULGIN.

MEGALITH - A huge stone that forms a prehistoric monument or part of the construction work of ancient peoples, as in a stone circle or chamber tomb.

MERCURY - The closest planet to the Sun in our solar system. It is named for the Roman god, who was (among other things) the messenger of the gods and the guide of souls to the underworld. Mercury rules both astrologically and magically over all forms of mental activity, communication, travel and commerce. Its traditional metal is also called mercury, or "quicksilver" because it is liquid at room temperature. Mercury is also an alchemical principle in a trinity with Sulphur and Salt. In this trinity, Mercury is the dynamic, vitalizing, transforming quality bridging the essential quality that is the Sulphur and the manifested form or physical matrix that is the Salt.

See ALCHEMY, ENERGY and HIEROGLYPHIC MONAD.

MOON - The natural satellite of a planet or other celestial body, but especially the Earth's moon. Long a symbol of dreams, magic, romantic love and other forms of madness. The Moon rules both astrologically and magically over the subconscious, feelings and emotions, sensations, changes and fluctuations, women and the general public. On July 20, 1969 e.v., astronaut Neil Armstrong was the first known human to physically step foot on the Moon in a great moment for

Futurist and Surrealist dreams alike. Its traditional metal is silver.

See DREAMS.

MOONMILK - A limestone precipitate found in caves and made up of fine carbonate crystals. Moonmilk derives its name from its white color, creamy consistency and an early theory that it was produced by moon rays.

See GLOWWORM.

MUSAEUM CLAUSUM - The "Sealed Museum" is a tract containing a fictional inventory of "some remarkable books, antiquities, pictures and rarities of several kinds, scarce or never seen by any man now living" compiled by Sir Thomas Browne. The catalogue is divided into three sections listing imagined books, pictures and objects. These include a submarine herbal, a drawing of famous dwarfs and a large ostrich egg carved with a scene of the Battle of Three Kings. Written sometime between 1675 and 1682 e.v. (when Browne died) but not published until 1684.

MUSIQUE CONCRETE - Music combining electronically produced and recorded sound. This is, of course, very familar to us today when synthesizers and sampling are ubiquitous. However, this was not the case in the 1940s e.v. when such practices emerged in an atmosphere of experimentation. For the first time, composition of music was liberated from the inherent structures and limitations of traditional live instrumentation. With gramophone or radio as the media of expression, compositional forms reflecting the liberation from immediate time and space became possible. Such compositions are the musical equivalent of collage or assemblage. Today, the most generic dance remixes make use of the methodologies of musique concrete but the transtemporal and transspatial aims have become less pronounced or intentional. Of course, they may be easily retrieved by those willing to do so.

See ANALOGUE SYNTHESIS, ANS SYNTHESIZER, ART OF NOISES, CUT-UP TECHNIQUE, FOUND RECORDINGS, GLITCH, GRANULAR SYNTHESIS, INDUSTRIAL CULTURE and SIDEREAL SOUND.

N

FRIEDRICH NIETZSCHE · German philosopher, also known as Dionysus.

Nietzsche's philosophy is rooted in what he called "perspectivism" or the idea that all meaning or conceptual schemes depend upon perspective and that "Truth" can only be partially arrived at by integrating multiple perspectives (though not all perspectives are held to be equally valid). Relatedly, Nietzsche was extremely critical of normative morality, though he did assert a higher morality for Higher Men (see below). Coming to the conclusion that common morals do not nurture the best in Man, he famously declared the death of God as a credible source for absolute moral principles or guidance.

Nietzsche's philosophy is best known for two key concepts: the Will to Power and the *Übermensch* (meaning Superman, Overman or Higher-Being). The idea behind the Will to Power is that each unique entity strives to extend its force and be master over all space against all that resists its extension. This is the primary drive. As entities encounter similar efforts from other entities, they come to arrangements for living with those others with whom they are sufficiently related in affinity and purpose. The Übermensch is a major goal of becoming that humanity might set for itself in that process, attained by the Self-overcoming of the human in an aristocratic vision that is ontological rather than merely political and hereditary. Moreover, the Übermensch and the quest for it provide meaning to this world and life in it rather than diverting human attention and energies into otherworldly after-life fantasy schemes.

If Nietzsche's philosophy can be summarized with any accuracy in a short book entry such as this, the best bet is with the following quote from *The Antichrist*:

"What is good? -- Whatever augments the feeling of power, the will to power, power itself, in man...What is evil? -- Whatever springs from weakness...What is happiness? -- The feeling that power increases -- that resistance is being overcome...Not contentment, but more power; not peace at any price, but war; not virtue, but efficiency (virtue in the Renaissance sense, virtù, virtue free of the taint of morality)...The weak and the botched shall perish: first principle of our charity. And one should help them to it...What is more harmful than any vice? -- Practical sympathy for the botched and the weak -- Christianity..."

Of course, like anyone promoting an Individualist and life-affirming philosophy (Crowley, Rand, LaVey, et cetera), both Nietzsche and his ideas are routinely misquoted, misrepresented and demonized. It did not help that his sister was a Nazi and made a deal with the state for financial support of the Nietzsche archive in return for a bastardized philosophical pseudo-endorsement of Hitlerian ideals.

See ANTICHRIST, ESCHATON, FUTURISM and THELEMA.

THE NIGHT OF THE HUNTER - A film from 1955 e.v. in which actor Robert Mitchum plays itinerant preacher and serial killer Rev. Harry Powell. After doing time for a lesser offense, Powell seeks out and marries the widow of his cell mate so as to find the hidden money from a bank robbery. After killing his new wife, Powell becomes guardian of the children who know the secret of where the money is and the story goes from there. The film and the novel from which it derives (by Davis Grubb) were based on the true story of Harry Powers, who lured lonely women through personal ads and murdered them for their money.

P

PAN · Greek god of wilderness, forests and pastures, hunters, shepherds and flocks. Lecherous companion of the Nymphs, Pan is depicted as a horned man with goat-like legs. In the 18th century e.v., a nobleman named Benjamin Hyett took up residence outside the Cotswold village of Painswick and decided to create an annual procession dedicated to Pan which lasted for many years.

See ALEX SANDERS.

PARANOIAC-CRITICAL METHOD · Visionary method developed by Salvador Dali for creating his illusory, double-image paintings. As Dali was not one given to plain talk, it can be difficult to understand and even more difficult to apply. In a way, it is similar to pareidolia, the phenomenon that accounts for seeing images in clouds, ink blots or stains. However, Paranoiac-Critical Method differs from pareidolia in that one learns to see alternative scenes and images not in suggestive, amorphous shapes or substances but in defined scenes and images such as non-abstract paintings, photographs and the world around us.

However, to find one's way into this state of vision, one might begin practicing with ordinary pareidolia supplemented with the regular viewing of optical illusions · particularly of the double-image type (such as the famous vase or chalice framed between two faces). Next, practice looking at paintings and photographs from a distance and/or in dim light. Look for alternative images. Do the same during twilight walks, scanning your environment to see what might be there. As you build up the knack, try applying full Paranoiac-Critical Method to well-lit objects and environments.

Of course, it should be noted that the paranoid-critical state greatly resembles the mental state of some very dysfunctional people. Dali claimed that the difference between him and a madman was that he was not mad. The poet Rimbaud spoke of the need to become a visionary through a long, boundless and systematic disorganization of all the senses. Surrealism's Self-appointed Pope, Andre Breton, was inspired by Rimbaud's language and spoke of a descent into the hidden places and forbidden territory within. What Dali seems to be saying is that he was able to accomplish some of what Rimbaud and Breton alluded to by perceiving in the manner of the mad while simultaneously maintaining a functional perspective.

See SALVADOR DALI, LIMINALITY, SURREALISM and SYNESTHESIA.

ARVO PÄRT - Estonian composer of classical and sacred music. Pärt uses a Self-developed method of composition that he calls *tintinnabuli* (from the Latin word for bells) based upon a minimalist and precise relationship between melody and accompaniment.

See ALAIN PRESENCER and JILL PURCE.

PENETRALIA - The innermost parts of a building; a secret or hidden place.

PERFORMANCE - A 1970 e.v. film directed by Donald Cammell and Nicolas Roeg that concerns an urban gangster named Chas (James Fox) that is forced to hide out in the basement apartment of a large townhouse owned by faded, reclusive rock star Turner (Mick Jagger). The desperate Chas and bored Turner are each intrigued by the life of the other. Assorted varieties of hallucinogenic mushrooms grow around the property, cultivated by Turner's secretary and lover Pherber (Anita Pallenberg). Weird times happen and the film ends ambiguously. Noteworthy for an early popular culture mention of Hassan i Sabbah and the slogan "Nothing is True, Everything is Permitted".

See DONALD CAMMELL, PSILOCYBIN and NICOLAS ROEG.

PIETISM · Originally, a 17th-century e.v. German religious movement advocating a revival of the devotional ideal in the Lutheran Church. By extension, any system or approach that stresses the devotional in religious experience.

PIG · Swine, hog. An animal of the genus *sus* with a long broad snout and a thick, fat body covered with coarse bristles. Commonly, pigs are symbols of gluttony. In heraldry, however, the boar is a symbol of endurance and courage and may also signify ferocity in battle or skill in hunting. In Germany, the pig is a traditional symbol of good luck. The consumption of pork is forbidden in Judaism and Islam, which may be rooted in the association of the pig with the ancient Egyptian god Set.

ALAIN PRESENCER · Known for his 1981 e.v. album *The Singing Bowls of Tibet*, Presencer champions the simple, "primal sound" of these instruments as a means of consecrating space and providing a healing influence for those overdosed on what he calls the "cacophony" (derived from Greek for "bad sound") of urban life.

See ART OF NOISES, DRONE, ARVO PÄRT, JILL PURCE and SILENCE.

PSILOCYBIN · Compound produced within over 200 species of mushrooms and easily converted by the body into the powerful psychedelic psilocin, with effects comparable to those of LSD and DMT. Both psilocybin and psilocin were indeed first isolated by Albert Hoffman, who had earlier discovered LSD. However, the use of such mushrooms in shamanic and religious ritual spans history and the globe. The study of such rituals in Mexico by R. Gordon Wasson in the 1950s e.v. introduced "magic mushrooms" to the modern, industrialized world. Hoffman isolated the compounds a year after an article by Wasson was published in *Life* magazine.

Prior to his more well-known advocacy of LSD, Timothy Leary worked with psilocybin at Harvard along with Richard Alpert under the aegis of the Harvard Psilocybin Project. This was very academic and official, though there was some furor when the project later became more publicly known. In the project's Marsh Chapel Experiment (also known as the Good Friday Experiment), psilocybin was successfully used to induce (or amplify) religious experience.

Terence McKenna later advocated not just the use of psilocybin mushrooms but the reintroduction of a shamanic context for their use and understanding as catalysts of spiritual and cultural evolution.

See DMT, HARMALINE, LSD, TERENCE MCKENNA and SHAMANISM.

PSYCHOGEOGRAPHY · Psychogeography began in the Lettrist art and cultural movement and continued into Situationism. Simply put, it is the study of the effects of environments upon the psychology and behavior of people in those environments. We shape the environment and are in turn shaped by it in a reciprocal, spiral process.

Though the term pre-dates psychogeography in the sense that we are describing it here, we can use the elements of *ekistics* (coined by Konstantinos Apostolou Doxiadis from the Greek *oikos* for "home" or "habitat") to begin to understand the psychogeographical environment. The basic ekistic elements are Nature, Anthropos (Man), Society,

R

RAT · Long-tailed rodents resembling but larger than mice. The most common species are the black rat (*rattus rattus*) and the brown rat (*rattus norvegicus*). Rats reach sexual maturity beginning at three months and a pair of brown rats left unchecked can produce 2000 descendents in a year. The front teeth of rats grow at a rate of about five inches a year and must be worn down by continuous gnawing.

REMOTE VIEWING · Traditionally known as *clairvoyance* (from the French for "clear seeing") this is the practice of perception at a distance via some spiritual or mental faculty other than the immediate, known senses. The more plain, English term was applied by researchers Harold Puthoff and Russell Targ for the sake of experiments in military and intelligence applications.

See ASTRAL and SCRYING.

BOYD RICE · Dadaist, Social Darwinist, Satanist, Gnostic, tikiphile, girl group musicologist, prankster, writer, visual artist, actor and Industrial and Noise artist. Performs as both Boyd Rice and NON. If his career can be said to have an implicit, central organizing principle other than following his own bliss, it is in bridging the gap in Man's divided nature as shown in the title of his NON album *God & Beast*.

See ANTICHRIST, DADA, INDUSTRIAL CULTURE, FRIEDRICH NIETZSCHE, RUNES and TRANSGRESSIVE ART.

NICOLAS ROEG · English director and cinematographer known for such films as *Performance*, *The Man Who Fell to Earth* and *Eureka*, and for often taking a nonlinear, mosaic approach to the arrangement of scenes.

See DONALD CAMMELL, EUREKA and PERFORMANCE.

RUNES · The characters of several alphabets (or, more properly, *futharks*) used by the ancient Scandinavians and other Germanic peoples.

As usual, though, there is much more to it. The word "rune" generally means "mystery" or "secret" and each rune has ever-deeper levels of symbolic meaning in addition to its semiotic function as a letter. Mythologically, the runes were discovered by Odin during a shamanistic, ritual sacrifice of Himself to Himself in which He obtained the knowledge of them and their powers. As such, the runes were not merely the writing alphabet of the Germanic peoples but were (are) powerful tools for casting enchantments and divinations.

For this reason, a magical spell, song or even poem may also be more generally called a rune.

See DARKNESS, SNOW and YEW.

S

DONATIEN ALPHONSE FRANCOIS DE SADE · More well-known as simply the Marquis de Sade, whose name is the source of the term "sadism". Sade is known as something of a philosopher-pornographer, using erotic novels such as *Justine* and *The 120 Days of Sodom* to depict acts of blasphemy, criminality, sexual perversion and violence in accord with a libertine philosophy of absolute freedom from religion, morality and law. Unsurprisingly, he spent nearly half of his life in various prisons and the Charenton asylum.

Despite both this and being an aristocrat, the Marquis was also an active revolutionary who wrote political pamphlets and tracts and served as a delegate to the National Convention during the French Revolution. Known for his radical positions, he ironically lost his place and was imprisoned (again) due to accusations of moderatism for his critical opinions of Robespierre and the Reign of Terror · but that is politics for you.

In his last years, the director of Charenton allowed Sade to stage several of his plays with his fellow inmates as actors, until these were ordered stopped by the government. After centuries of shame, his descendents revived the title of Marquis along with family interest in his work in the 20th century e.v.

See SALO, SODOMY and TRANGRESSIVE ART.

SALO - Or the *120 Days of Sodom*, from the Marquis de Sade's book of the same name, *Salo* is a 1975 e.v. film by Pier Paolo Pasolini that updates and transposes Sade's story to the days of Fascist Italy. The film also draws structural and philosophical inspiration from Dante Alighieri's *Divine Comedy* and Friedrich Nietzsche's *On the Genealogy of Morals*.

The story is essentially the same as Sade's, with four powerful men - the Duke, Bishop, Magistrate and President - abducting a collection of young men and women and taking them to a remote palace with the aim of subjecting them to every form of psychological and sexual torture. The placement of these events in more recent times, however, perhaps makes the themes of political corruption and abuse of power more relatable and this is enhanced by the film medium's ability to graphically depict scenes of violence and sadism.

See FRIEDRICH NIETZSCHE, OSTIA, DONATIEN ALPHONSE FRANCOIS DE SADE and TRANSGRESSIVE ART.

ALEX SANDERS - Self-proclaimed "King of the Witches" and founder of the Alexandrian tradition or lineage of Wicca or witchcraft. Born Orrell Alexander Carter and later using the craft name Verbius, Sanders worked as a medium and healer in Spiritualist churches but claimed to have been initiated into witchcraft by his grandmother. He also claimed that she introduced him to Aleister Crowley. Whether or not this is true, he was later initiated into a coven of the tradition and lineage started by Gerald Gardner (Gardnerian) before starting his own.

The Gardnerian and Alexandrian traditions are quite similar but do have some differences. Gardner and Sanders were both influenced by Aleister Crowley, but it seems that Sanders was more so and the Alexandrian rituals tend to be more closely aligned with ceremonial magic of the Crowleyan type. The Alexandrians also tend to be more open and eclectic, generally. Anecdotal, subjective accounts of the feeling of Alexandrian circles describe the energy as more fiery than the earthy Gardnerian atmospheres.

See PAN and THELEMA.

SCATOLOGY · An interest in or preoccupation with excrement and excretion. May be expressed as a sexual fetish, psychological obsession or simply as a theme in art, literature or humor.

See ALCHEMY, FETISHISM and GOLD.

SCRYING · The seeking of visions by gazing into pools or bowls of water or of ink, crystal spheres, mirrors, fire, smoke or simply darkness. All of these provide external analogues for the dark waters of the subconscious, points of fixation for the trance state of psychic receptivity and screens upon which visions may be viewed.

See ASTRAL, DARKNESS, SIR JOHN DEE, ESOTERIC ORDER OF DAGON, SIR EDWARD KELLEY, REMOTE VIEWING and SHAMANISM.

SHAMANISM · The regular and direct engagement with the magical environment by a ritual technician commonly known to anthropologists as a shaman, but having local titles in the cultures in which they reside. The shaman usually provides services of healing, exorcism and magical defense (or attack) to the community.

It is important to further stress the immediacy of the shaman's experience. Songs, dances, psychoactive drugs and other ritual tools are used to perceive or travel to an "otherworld" or series of them as well as the unseen dimension of the shaman's familiar surroundings. In these realms, the shaman interacts and negotiates with a wide variety of spirits. Indeed, while a shaman may have a human teacher, most of their knowledge will come directly from the spirits. Shamans also habitually steal knowledge and power from spirits. Apparently, the spirits (sometimes) expect this and it can be an important part of a shaman's initiation.

An important myth to shatter regarding the subject is the image of the shaman as being a conservative figure full of traditionalist cliches. This may be so of a particular shaman but could not be farther from the truth when it comes to the spirit of the practice, itself. Yes, it is true that a shaman keeps cultural lore, presides over rites of passage and contributes to social cohesion in some ways like a priest. But remember that a shaman will also not hesitate to steal knowledge or power from the spirits.

The shaman is eminently practical. A story is recalled concerning a shaman who was taken into a city. He became excited at the idea of learning the songs for automobiles and airplanes. If cars and planes are part of the environment, the shaman wants to learn their songs. Indeed, there are strong connections between shamanism and technology through the history of metalsmithing.

It is worth mentioning two very different but complementary books here. The first is Mircea Eliade's *Shamanism*, which he calls the archaic techniques of ecstasy. This book catalogues shamanic lore from around the world. The other is *The Way of the Shaman* by Michael Harner, which introduces what Harner calls "core shamanism" as a methodology for utilizing basic and universal shamanic practices outside of any particular cultural context.

The insightful reader could surely use these two books in conjunction with leads from this book to create a personal, vital form of shamanic practice adapted to modern, urban, technological environments, if they so wished.

See ASTRAL, DMT, DRONE, DREAMS, HARMALINE, ISOLATIONISM, LIMINALITY, PSILOCYBIN, PSYCHOGEOGRAPHY, REMOTE VIEWING, SCRYING and VULTURE.

ALEXANDER SHULGIN · American chemist and pharmacologist who personally synthesized and tested over 230 psychoactive compounds. The fruits of these labors are recorded in his books *PIHKAL* (Phenethylamines I Have Known And Loved) and *TIHKAL* (the Tryptamines) written with his wife Ann. He is also credited with having introduced psychologists to MDMA (Ecstasy) as a therapeutic aid in the 1970s e.v. In his earlier career, Shulgin developed the first biodegradable pesticide, mexacarbate (trade name, Zectran).

See DMT, DOET and MDMA.

SIDEREAL SOUND · An approach to making audio works with the intention of impacting the listener from odd angles or unexpected viewpoints by exploiting possibilities for subtly manipulating the quality or experience of sound. Sidereal Sound in practice, then, is an attitude or aesthetic rather than any one, specific process or technology.

See BINAURAL BEATS, DEEP LISTENING, LIMINALITY, MUSIQUE CONCRETE and SUBLIMINAL.

SILENCE · The absence of sound. Hush, quiet, noiselessness.

Silence was an important concept for William S. Burroughs, who felt that WORD was a virus. Symbiotic at best, parasitic at worst, but separate and alien. In the outer, he worked to "rub out" the Word through methods like the cut-up technique. In the inner, he was influenced by Carlos Castaneda's stress on the importance of stopping the compulsive internal dialogue. Castaneda said:

"The internal dialogue is what grounds people in the daily world. The world is such and such or so and so, only because we talk to ourselves about its being such and such and so and so. The passageway into the world of shamans opens up after the warrior has learned to shut off his internal dialogue."

For Burroughs, this tied into his conception of migration into SPACE. He insisted that you can not take WORD into SPACE and felt that inner silence was key to the process.

On the other hand, Terence McKenna also said that the world was made of language but sought ways to use that. Metaphysically, it might be useful to compare what is said in the entry for "Unknowns" (below) about Darkness and Light with the elements of Silence and Sound.

See WILLIAM S. BURROUGHS, DARKNESS and UNKNOWNS.

EDITH SITWELL · English poet and Dame of the Most Excellent Order of the British Empire. In addition to her poetry and books on Queens Elizabeth I and Victoria, Sitwell also wrote the popular *The English Eccentrics*. On the subject of eccentricity, she said:

"Eccentricity is not, as some would believe, a form of madness. It is often a kind of innocent pride, and the man of genius and the aristocrat are frequently regarded as eccentrics because genius and aristocrat are entirely unafraid of and uninfluenced by the opinions and vagaries of the crowd."

SLEEP · Condition of rest for the mind and body in which there is little or no conscious thought, sensation or movement. During sleep, the body performs maintenance, growth and rejuvenation of the immune, nervous, skeletal, and muscular systems while the mind does the same through memory processing and dreaming.

There is an Indian practice called *yoga nidra* that is referred to as yogic sleep because it involves entering very deep states of relaxation while maintaining conscious awareness. In Daoism, there is a tradition of practices for cultivating and circulating internal energies while sleeping. The legendary master Chen Tuan, known as the Sleeping Immortal, is said to have engaged in these sleeps for months at a time.

See DREAMS.

SNOW · Particles of water vapor which become frozen in the upper air and fall to the ground as soft, white, crystalline flakes. These flakes take a wide variety of forms, so the crystals are often said to be unique and the snowflake is sometimes used as a symbol or label for uniqueness.

Also slang for cocaine as well as the visual static appearing on dead channels on old televisions. This latter was sometimes used by the Industrial Magicians of bygone, pre-digital days for scrying purposes.

See MAGNETIC NORTH, RUNES and SCRYING.

SODOMY · Term usually referring to anal sexual intercourse but which has historically been applied to oral sex and even bestiality, as well; and to such acts among both heterosexual and homosexual practitioners. The name comes from the Biblical city of Sodom, described along with the city of Gomorrah as being exceedingly depraved and sinful.

See BLACK SUN, DONATIEN ALPHONSE FRANCOIS DE SADE, KUNDALINI and THELEMA.

SOLAR LODGE · California group active in the 1960s e.v. and based on the Thelemic teachings of Aleister Crowley. The story of the Solar Lodge began when a woman named Jean Brayton ("Soror Capricornus") was given an initiation by a man named Ray Burlingame ("Frater Aquarius"), who was a IX° initiate of the Ordo Templi Orientis (OTO) and later authorized her to initiate others. Burlingame had no charter from the OTO to provide initiations, though, so the Solar Lodge was considered a rogue group. At one point, however, the Solar Lodge had over fifty members and owned several homes and businesses, as well as a ranch in the Sonoran desert. The group eventually ran into trouble over charges of child abuse and were later linked to Charles Manson, though the facts in both scandals are disputed.

See BLACK SUN and THELEMA.

SOLSTICE · When the sun reaches the farthest point either north or south of the equator. The north solstice marks the passage from spring to summer in the northern hemisphere and from fall to winter in the southern hemisphere. The south solstice marks the passage from fall to winter in the northern hemisphere and from spring to summer in the southern hemisphere. The north and south solstices occur in June and December, respectively. The word "solstice" derives from Latin meaning "sun stands still", as it appears to do in having reached its farthest point in one direction before reversing its apparent movement. Thus, the term can also refer more poetically to any turning point or point of culmination.

See EQUINOX and LIMINALITY.

SONGS OF MALDOROR · French novel (*Les Chants de Maldoror*) by the Comte de Lautréamont (pseudonym of Isidore-Lucien Ducasse). More blasphemous, violent and obscene than the Marquis de Sade, and far more imaginative. Indeed, Lautréamont was hailed by the Surrealists who came over half a century later as a master and progenitor.

He speaks directly within the text about the dangerous philosophical journey that is about to ensue and the reader of the cantos is warned from the start:

"God grant that the reader, emboldened and having become at present as fierce as what he is reading, find, without loss of bearings, his way, his wild and treacherous passage through the desolate swamps of these sombre, poison-soaked pages; for, unless he should bring to his reading a rigorous logic and a sustained mental effort at least as strong as his distrust, the lethal fumes of this book shall dissolve his soul as water does sugar."

And then the world is introduced to Maldoror, antichrist and antihero, misanthrope and murderer. His story has no real plot, he restlessly wanders through places, events and situations while Lautréamont paints scenes of poetic and creative evil that are almost more expressionistic than narrative. Indeed, Maldoror does not even have a fixed form, being sometimes a spirit, a man or even a great octopus who wrestles God.

As mentioned, *Maldoror* was a great influence upon the Surrealists and both Salvador Dali and Rene Magritte did illustrations for editions of the book. Hans Bellmer also did illustrations based on scenes from the story. Japanese director Shûji Terayama made a short film inspired by the text in 1977 e.v.

See ANTICHRIST, SALVADOR DALI, SURREALISM and TRANSGRESSIVE ART.

AUSTIN OSMAN SPARE - English artist and Magician born in London at the end of the 19th century e.v. His work with the subconscious provides a counterpoint to the superconscious focus of Aleister Crowley, with whom Spare was briefly affiliated.

At the age of 12, Spare began taking night classes at the Lambeth School of Art and later took a job at a company that made posters. He was recommended for a scholarship to the Royal College of Art and enjoyed great success early on. However, Spare turned his back on the formal art world and spent many of his later years in great poverty, painting portraits in pubs.

Spare was contemporary to the birth of Surrealism and, while he was not affiliated with the movement, his work was closely aligned with it on the subject of automatism. He produced a large body of fantastic automatic drawings and also wrote a short text on the subject. In this text, he said that:

"This means of vital expression releases the fundamental static truths which are repressed by education and customary habit and lie dormant in the mind. It is the means of becoming courageously individual; it implies spontaneity and disperses the cause of unrest and ennui."

Spare and his work experienced a revival in the 1970s thanks to Kenneth Grant, who wrote about Spare in his books as well as publishing some of Spare's own material. This opened the way for Spare's magical ideas and practices to be adopted by groups such as the Illuminates of Thanateros and Temple ov Psychick Youth, which popularized them even further over the next two decades.

See ILLUMINATES OF THANATEROS, LIMINALITY, SURREALISM and ZOS KIA CULTUS.

STEVEN STAPLETON · English musician and artist, main man behind Nurse With Wound and the United Dairies record label. Stapleton's creative output is astonishingly · even frighteningly · prolific. Nurse With Wound have produced nearly a hundred albums as of this writing, while also appearing on various compilations or collaborating with other groups and artists. As "Babs Santini", Stapleton is also an accomplished visual artist. As if all of this were not enough, he has also created a number of environments and filled them with handmade and restored furnishings at his Cooloorta compound in Ireland. We should all strive to be like Steven Stapleton.

See INDUSTRIAL CULTURE and SURREALISM.

STAR-SPONGE VISION · A vision experienced by Aleister Crowley in 1916 e.v. He described it in comments on the Book of the Law and in his autobiography as follows:

"I was on a retirement in a cottage overlooking Lake Pasquaney in New Hampshire. I lost consciousness of everything but a universal space in which were innumerable bright points, and I realized this as a physical representation of the universe, in what I may call its essential structure. I exclaimed, 'Nothingness with twinkles!' I concentrated upon this vision, with the result that the void space which had been the principal element of it diminished in importance; space appeared to be ablaze, yet the radiant points were not confused, and I thereupon

completed my sentence with the exclamation, 'but what twinkles!'

"The next stage of this vision led to an identification of the blazing points with the stars of the firmament, with ideas, souls, etc. I perceived also that each star was connected by a ray of light with each other star. In the world of ideas each thought possessed a necessary relation with each other thought; each such relation is of course a thought in itself; each such ray is itself a star. It is here that the logical difficulty first presents itself. The seer has a direct perception of infinite series. Logically, therefore, it would appear as if the entire space must be filled up with a homogeneous blaze of light. This however is not the case. The space is completely full and yet the monads which fill it are perfectly distinct. The ordinary reader might well exclaim that such statements exhibit symptoms of mental confusion."

See CHAOS and THELEMA.

KARLHEINZ STOCKHAUSEN · German experimental composer who worked with a variety of styles such as musique concrete, electronics and drone. Spatialization was an important concept for Stockhausen and his music was sometimes performed in a specially created spherical auditorium with the audience in the center and surrounded by rings of loudspeakers along the interior wall.

See DRONE, JILL PURCE and LA MONTE YOUNG.

IGOR STRAVINSKY · Innovative Russian pianist, composer and conductor known for the avant-garde yet explicitly pagan ballet *The Rite of Spring*, which originally featured choreography by Vaslav Nijinsky and costumes and sets by Nicholas Roerich.

See EQUINOX.

SUBLIMINAL · Below the threshold of consciousness or apprehension.

Subconscious. Too slight to be perceived, as in a subliminal stimulus. Commonly refers to either sound content mixed into a recording below the level of ordinary hearing or visual material presented more quickly than can ordinarily register consciously.

See LIMINALITY and SIDEREAL SOUND.

SUN RA · Stage name and philosophical persona of innovative jazz musician Herman Poole Blount. He told of an experience of being spiritually transported during religious meditation to a planet that he identified as Saturn, where he spoke with alien beings. As Sun Ra, he claimed to be from Saturn, himself. In this, he was an early example of Afrofuturism and an influence on later artists such as George Clinton and Rammellzee.

SURREALISM · The word "surrealist" was coined by poet Guillaume Apollinaire in the preface to his play *Les Mamelles de Tirésias*, first performed in 1917 e.v. Surrealism as a movement, however, did not emerge until the next decade and it did not initially do so through the arts as one might expect. It emerged through mediumistic seances.

It began with a small number of young writers meeting in the apartment of André Breton for an experiment. The group wanted to try the methods of trance employed by Spiritualist mediums but from a psychological rather than mystical orientation. They wanted to contact the unconscious. This "period of the sleeping fits" resulted in automatic writing and drawing as well as spoken material. When Surrealism became an actual movement and Breton started writing manifestos, he defined Surrealism directly as:

"Pure psychic automatism, by which one seeks to express, be it verbally, in writing, or in any other manner, the real working of the mind. Dictated by the unconsciousness, in the absence of any control exercised by reason, and free from aesthetic or moral preoccupations."

From there, Surrealism got big and complicated. It washed over the

20th century and its meaning has now been degraded to a fancy word for general weirdness. However, it is possible to peer through the clouds of words and determine two essential and related Surreal aims: the liberation of Desire and the attainment of the Super-Reality (as "surreal" means "beyond the real").

The liberation of Desire involves transgression or the breaking of taboos when needed as any form of erotic insurrection must but it must also seek out a pure and honest place from which to act rather than merely reacting. It must primarily seek to invoke *l'amour fou* or "mad love" and the deepest desires and deepest springs of libidinal energy.

There is a deeply erotic dimension to Alchemy and its imagery which appealed to the Surrealists because the weaving of forces and sacred marriages depicted in alchemical literature are suggestive of both sexuality and the larger reunification of the realms of conscious and unconscious experience within the Super-Reality. Of this Breton said:

"I believe in the future resolution of these two states, dream and reality, which are seemingly so contradictory, into a kind of absolute reality, a surreality, if one may so speak."

While Surrealist art is certainly meant to convey beauty - intense and radical forms of it - it goes beyond the usual approach of traditional art in conveying that beauty. The creation of a work of Surrealist art is an exploration. Desire must be freed and/or some portion of the Super-Reality must be glimpsed or expressed.

For these reasons, the Surrealists were interested in the art of children, primitive peoples and the mentally ill for both the purity of their visions and unselfconscious expressions. They were interested in the ideas and imagery of Magic and Alchemy for the technology and paradigms that would facilitate uniting the worlds.

In these efforts, Surrealism did not depend upon the trance states of the initial seances only. A number of techniques were developed for introducing random or otherwise novel and inspiring elements into the creative process. A few useful methods such as the cut-up technique, decalcomania and paranoiac-critical method have separate entries in this book.

Surrealism is applicable to all facets of existence. Indeed, it must be. While everyone knows about Surrealist painting, sculpture, writing and film, it also has obvious applications to psychology. These could theoretically be even further extended to something like medicine via the link between mind and body. The original Surrealist movement also had a political dimension but fell into the trap of authoritarianism (Communism) like the Futurists had (Fascism), while Anarchism would seem the much better fit.

These are just a few broad examples, imagination is the only limit here. While some Surrealist aims and aesthetics had great influence in shaping the arts and media of today, so much of its potential remains untapped.

See ALCHEMY, CUT-UP TECHNIQUE, DECALCOMANIA, DREAMS, MAX ERNST, ALFRED JARRY, ROBERTO MATTA, PARANOIAC-CRITICAL METHOD, SONGS OF MALDOROR, AUSTIN OSMAN SPARE, YVES TANGUY and TRANSGRESSIVE ART.

SYNESTHESIA - Experience in which one type of stimulus produces a secondary, subjective sensation. Examples could include a specific sound also evoking a specific color (or vice versa) or a pairing of sound and tactile sensation. A similar experience is known as *ideasthesia*, an example of which would be a specific number or letter of the alphabet also evoking the sensation of a color.

See ANS SYNTHESIZER.

T

YVES TANGUY · Surrealist painter who often combined fantastic scenes with minimal landscapes, notably beach shorelines. Untrained as an artist and originally a sailor, Tanguy only decided to begin painting after being impressed by the work of Giorgio de Chirico.

See LIMINALITY, ROBERTO MATTA and SURREALISM.

THELEMA · Philosophical, religious and magical system for the Aeon of Horus, developed by Aleister Crowley as its Magus. Its essential and fundamental statement is *Liber AL vel Legis* or the "Book of the Law", dictated to Crowley by an entity called Aiwass in Cairo, Egypt, during the spring of 1904 e.v. The word *Thelema* is a Greek term for Will.

An important precursor to Crowley's system can be found in the fictional, counter-monastic Abbey of Thélème described by the 16th-century French writer Francois Rabelais. Of the Thélèmites, it is written:

"All their life was spent not in laws, statutes, or rules, but according to their own free will and pleasure. They rose out of their beds when they thought good; they did eat, drink, labour, sleep, when they had a mind to it and were disposed for it. None did awake them, none did offer to constrain them to eat, drink, nor to do any other thing; for so had Gargantua established it. In all their rule and strictest tie of their

order there was but this one clause to be observed,

"Do What Thou Wilt..."

"Do what thou wilt shall be the whole of the Law. Love is the law, love under will." became the watchwords of Crowley's doctrine and he would later establish his own Abbey of Thelema in Sicily, of course.

Being something of an over-achiever, Crowley's voluminous writings contain a number of what Daoists would call "side roads" such as qabalistic meanderings, buddhoid attempts at Self-annihilation and pseudo-Gnostic religious pageantry. Unfortunately, these "side roads" can provide many with comfortable and distracting havens from the real and serious work of Thelema, the core of which consists of Knowledge and Conversation of the Holy Guardian Angel, discovery and doing of one's True Will and the manifestation and safeguarding of the Law of Liberty.

Crowley's use of the term "Knowledge and Conversation of the Holy Guardian Angel" derives from the famous Abramelin Operation, a magical retreat described in Abraham of Worms' grimoire *The Book of Abramelin*, to which the reader is referred. However, even in pre-Judeo-Christian times, Classical Magicians spoke of a personal Hermes, or messenger from the Gods. We might relate this to a magical relationship with the more well-known *Genius* of the Romans or the *Daimon* of the Greeks (of which Socrates spoke).

We might think of this Angel, then, as our "Higher" or Superconscious Self as described by Roberto Assagioli - or as our core or essential Self clothed in material from the Superconscious. This Self exists as one pole of our psyche with the other being the everyday persona or character with which we normally identify. Knowledge and Conversation between these two poles would be profoundly enlightening once achieved. The Magician might then use what it learns from the Angel to remake the persona or character - which is usually largely the accidental creation of external influences - into a truer and more concentrated image of the Self.

This concentrated state of Being results in a commensurate focus of the Will. Crowley used to say that it was absolutely necessary to achieve Knowledge and Conversation of the Holy Guardian Angel before you could do any *real* Magic. Part of the rationale behind such a statement is simply that you have to be in tune with who you really are and what you really want before you can consciously work to make the right things happen. Roberto Assagioli, again, has much to say about Will and his works are strongly recommended for the modern Thelemite.

Finally, the Law of Liberty as expressed in Crowley's most explicit political statement, *Liber LXXVII (OZ)*, defines the conditions of freedom necessary for a society of Individuals who are doing their Will. Crowley provides a simple list of basic rights and implies that they derive from the divinity of Man and the sovereign imperative to do his Will. He was never really able to flesh out Thelemic political theory more fully, but it is fortunate that more rigorous and supportive libertarian movements were emerging in Crowley's day and are now quite mature and sophisticated (even if still not quite as popular as one might wish). The Law of Liberty remanifests the culture of Rabelais' Abbey on a societal scale.

Of course, the thing for which Thelema was originally most notorious was the promotion of Sex Magick (as Crowley spelled it). This term can actually be applied to four types of activity. The most abstract of these would be the illustration of an alchemical *hierogamos* ("sacred marriage") between the Male and Female principles or archetypes. This might be more properly referred to as Sex Mysticism, though it may provide a context for the other forms.

The most immediately practical application of Sex Magick is the use of orgasm as an amplifier of whatever aim or focus is held firmly in the mind at the climactic moment. A more extended project is the exploration of sexuality and deep desire as a form of increasing Self-knowledge and in nourishing or transcending aspects of the persona or character as willed. These activities may be pursued outside of the strictly archetypal Male-Female *hierogamos* - as they certainly were by Crowley, himself - and the use of orgasm-as-amplifier may even be best employed as a solo operation.

These three types of Sex Magick could all be classed as Sex-as-Magick, while the fourth would be more accurately classed as Magick-as-Sex. This Mystery is rarely explored, though it is implicit in the Book of the Law. Here, the Magician's operations and experiences may be seen as a form of sexual intercourse between him- or her-Self and the continuum of Everything Else personified as a lover. This perspective can unite and add new depth to the other three Sex Magick forms.

See CEFALU, SIR JOHN DEE, EQUINOX, ESCHATON, FUTURISM, SIR EDWARD KELLEY, FRIEDRICH NIETZSCHE, ONAN, QABALA, SODOMY and STAR-SPONGE VISION.

TIAMAT - Mesopotamian Goddess of the primordial Chaos and saltwater. In her matings with Abzu, the mingling of salt and fresh waters, she is the mytho-metaphysical Mother of all things.

However, reflecting the ambivalent nature of Chaos (or, rather, of attitudes toward it), Tiamat is also the Mother of Monsters such as Exalted Serpent, Hairy One, Big Weather-Beast, Scorpion-Man, Fish-Man and others who (as directed by their Mother) sought to overthrow the younger gods of order and civilization (also Tiamat's children). In this, Tiamat is also comparable in spirit to the later Typhon of the Greeks.

See HAKIM BEY and CHAOS.

TRANSGRESSIVE ART - Art that results in varying degrees of shock or outrage by transgressing the morals, values, beliefs or expectations of its audience. Outside of the aims of Dada and later filmmaker Nick Zedd's "Cinema of Transgression", trangressive art is not restricted to a particular movement or style. It is applicable to all forms of art and its expressions may be found in a variety of times and places. The transgression is usually intentional but may be accidental as the "rules" can vary so widely according to time and place, and what is actually transgressive may even be hard to determine.

For example, true transgressive art is unlikely to be found in the formal, established art world, which has its own easy and expected targets to "transgress" - though even these are now abused more out of perfunctory snark than any real feeling. Mocking Christianity, as an example, is pretty much beating a fossilized horse these days, while mocking Judaism or Islam might be more risky. Many more examples could be made but we would hate to possibly offend the reader.

Ultimately, the best transgressive art probably does not come primarily from the iconoclasm or blasphemy motivated even by actual anger or contempt (though these are certainly valuable) but rather from the sincere passion of true heresy, the genuine love of something currently forbidden or shockingly new.

See HAKIM BEY, WILLIAM S. BURROUGHS, DADA, HERMANN NITSCH, BOYD RICE, DONATIEN ALPHONSE FRANCOIS DE SADE, SALO and SONGS OF MALDOROR.

TWILIGHT LANGUAGE - A subtle and complex form of communication with multiple layers of meaning, some of which may only be interpreted by those "in the know" or through special forms of perception and interpretation.

The actual term "twilight language" first applies to Hindu and Buddhist tantric writings. The word "tantra" is itself an example as it refers to weaving and can thus be applied in different contexts to a text, a ritual, a magical spell or sexual intercourse. As very simple examples, esoteric teachings are encoded visually in mandalas and iconography, gesturally in *mudra* hand signs and numerically in text or any of the above. Each of these represents a door leading into further depths of meaning that may be communicated instantly (and permanently in works of art) by these simpler mnemonics.

This is very similar to the literature of Alchemy, which actually takes the idea much further. Alchemical writings not only contain heavy doses of symbolism in a variety of forms but may even be presented entirely in allegory. However, the legendary psychologist Carl Gustav

Jung's writings on Alchemy assert that its White Lions, Red Eagles, Death's Heads and so on go beyond mere code to become a true twilight language expressing aspects and processes of the deep psyche. This is greatly elaborated upon by Jung's disciple Marie-Louise von Franz in a number of her books.

Next, we can also consider Surrealist art as an even more thorough form of twilight language when we consider Surrealism's aim to transcend the dualism of conscious and subconscious experience within the Super-Reality. Moreover, some Surrealists were directly inspired by Alchemy and incorporated historical alchemical symbolism into their work, notably Max Ernst.

Finally, the term "Twilight Language" is also applied to a conspiracy theory developed by one James Shelby Downard who insisted that critical events are effected or manipulated to act out alchemical symbolism in real life and on a grand scale to influence the world. Examples include the detonation of the first atomic bomb (Destruction of Primordial Matter) and the assassination of John F. Kennedy (Death of the White King). In addition to alchemical themes, Downard's form of the Twilight Language consists of linking personal and place names as well as significant numbers. This kind of thing can also be seen in talk of occult, Satanic or "Illuminati" symbolism allegedly being used in popular culture and entertainment as some kind of psychological manipulation or mind control.

Of course, all of the entries in this book and the connections between them can also be seen as a form of Twilight Language and an example for elaboration and development, and hence this entry supplies the book's title.

See ALCHEMY, MAX ERNST, LIMINALITY and SURREALISM.

U

UNKNOWNS · In mathematics, equations may hold unknown quantities or variables. In life there are many similar unknown quantities or variables, mysteries, uncertainties, and ambiguities that may be less readily soluble. Indeed, quantum mechanics even has an Uncertainty Principle that describes the established place of such obscurity at the most fundamental level of reality.

Aleister Crowley wrote an essay on the duality of doubt or inquiry (which he called the Hunchback · ?) and revelation or realization (which he called the Soldier · !). Crowley points out that the Answer (!) to one Question (?) may only satisfy immediately, as it leads us into a new perspective where we may perceive more Questions (???). Questions are often ever-proliferating Quests. If we really look at this constantly regenerating and fecund state of affairs, we might perceive that we do not so much shine Light *into* Darkness with our inquiries but instead create Light *out of* Darkness · while creating even more Darkness out of the Light.

Relatedly, we can profitably include various unknowns into our Magic to provide a doorway for the unexpected and serendipitous. This was, of course, the operating principle underlying many of the techniques of Surrealism.

See DARKNESS, GLITCH and SURREALISM.

V

PAUL VAUGHAN · British journalist known for presenting art and science programs for radio and narrating many television science documentaries for the British Broadcasting Corporation, notably the series *Horizon* which Vaughan narrated from 1968 to 1995 e.v.

THE VELVET UNDERGROUND · Groundbreaking band from New York formed by Lou Reed and John Cale. Reed came from a garage band background while Cale came from a more classical one and was affiliated with the Fluxus arts movement. This mixture of influences, styles and skills caused the Velvet Underground to be a unique and mutant birth, unlike anything seen so far.

It also certainly did not hurt when they became attached to pop artist Andy Warhol and his community. Warhol made the Velvet Underground something of a house band for the scene at his Factory studio and included them in the Exploding Plastic Inevitable events. These latter combined live performances by the band, dancers and performance artists while Warhol films were projected over all of the action and the whole thing was rounded out with early technical light shows.

Commenting on the group's influence, musical innovator Brian Eno said that while the first Velvet Underground album may have initially sold only 30,000 copies, everyone who bought one of those 30,000 copies had probably started a band.

See INDUSTRIAL CULTURE, ANGUS MACLISE, WARHOL SUPERSTARS and LA MONTE YOUNG.

VIRUS · Archaically, a poison or venom, and by extension, any corrupting or poisoning influence of mind and character. In biology and medicine, any of a group of ultramicroscopic or submicroscopic infective agents, variously regarded as living organisms and as complex proteins, capable of multiplying in connection with living cells and that cause various diseases.

A virus essentially consists of information (DNA or RNA) that invades a cell and hijacks the mechanisms of that cell to replicate its information and reproduce itself. For this reason, the term has also been applied to nefarious programs that can infect the software or data files of a computer · the computer virus. In the theory of memetics, viral models are also applied to the spread and evolution of units of culture such as ideas, beliefs, behaviors, technologies, fads and so on. These units are known as "memes".

In our present cybernetic, hypermemetic and emergingly biotechnological Information Age, viral models have also become increasingly popular among Magicians · particularly those of the Chaos Magic(k) persuasion · who attempt to use a broad range of perceptual and magical tools in the hacking, designing and empowerment of viral memes as they will.

See WILLIAM S. BURROUGHS, TERENCE HIGGINS TRUST, ILLUMINATES OF THANATEROS and SILENCE.

VULTURE · Any of a number of large birds of prey related to the eagles and hawks, with naked and usually brightly colored heads and dark plumage. Vultures live on carrion and are found in tropical and temperate regions. Often viewed with distaste due to their appearance, diet and even excretory habits as they urinate straight down their legs and tend to vomit when startled.

However, the urinating and baldness protect the vulture from harmful bacteria as it wades through carcasses feeding and the vomiting is a defense mechanism. Moreover, the vulture's feeding habits may also be viewed as cleansing for the environment that it inhabits. Indeed, the scientific name for the Turkey Vulture, *cathartes aura*, means "golden purifier" in Latin.

The practice of "sky burial" in Tibet and parts of China involves dismembering corpses and leaving them out in the open to vultures and other birds of prey and scavenging animals. A similar Zoroastrian practice involves placing corpses on stone structures called Dakhma, commonly referred to in English as "Towers of Silence" (though this is not the true meaning of the Persian word, whose origins are unclear).

Indeed, this may be the origin of the imagery attached to angels, these winged beings that carry the dead away to heaven. A room known as the "vulture shrine" is found in the ancient settlement of Çatal Hüyük in southern Anatolia (Turkey) which flourished 9,000 years ago. Goat skulls and wing bones from large species of vulture were found in a cave in Kurdistan used for burials by the Zawi Chemi people nearly 11,000 years ago and are thought to have been part of a ritual costume.

See ANGEL, DEATH, JACKAL and SHAMANISM.

W

WARHOL SUPERSTARS · While this term technically best applies to those appearing in his films, it can often be extended to the larger clique of actors, artists, poets, filmmakers, musicians, assistants, transsexuals and drag queens, drug enthusiasts and combinations thereof surrounding artist Andy Warhol at his Factory studio and other New York locales such as Max's Kansas City restaurant.

The Factory environment was managed by photographer Billy Name, who provided its silver decor, and poet Gerard Malanga, who taught Warhol about screen printing. Key members of the scene were Brigid Berlin, whose father was chairman of the Hearst Corporation, and Ondine, who was an important social nexus for how the whole group came together. Others in the early films included poet Taylor Mead, socialite-model Jane Holzer, the youthful Bebe Hansen (daughter of artist Al Hansen and later the mother of musician Beck), later cult film star Mary Woronov and the iconic Edie Sedgwick.

Joe Dallesandro starred in a number of the bigger projects that Paul Morrissey created for the Warhol brand and later worked with John Waters. Viva, now mother of actress Gaby Hoffman, was on the telephone with Warhol when he was shot by a more fringe member of the group, radical feminist Valerie Solanas. Some of the Factory crowd appear as partygoers in the film *Midnight Cowboy*.

See ANGUS MACLISE and VELVET UNDERGROUND.

WAVEFORM · The shape of a wave · such as sawtooth, sine, square, triangular · as can be imaged on an oscilloscope.

See GLOWWORM.

JOHANNA WENT · American performance artist with roots in the California punk scene of the 1970s e.v. Her dynamic performances make heavy use of a variety of handmade costumes. Went also had a cameo appearance as a Carnoburger employee in the film *The Doom Generation*.

See BLACK SUN and TRANSGRESSIVE ART.

WESTON·SUPER·MARE · Seaside resort town in Somerset, England. Subject of the song "Sunny Weston-super-Mare" by The Wurzels.

WHITE CLIFFS OF DOVER · These chalk cliffs along the English coastline face the narrowest part of the English Channel and thus France and the rest of Europe, and so may be considered the land's "face" in a symbolic or poetic sense. Britain's ancient name of "Albion" may be related to these cliffs as the word may mean "white" (as Latin *albus*) but may instead mean "world" · or both.

See WILLIAM BLAKE and OSTIA.

X

XENOPHILIA - Attraction to or love for the foreign, exotic, strange or outright alien.

See ESOTERIC ORDER OF DAGON.

Y

YEW · Common name of a number of evergreen, coniferous shrubs or trees in the genus *Taxus*. The European common yew (*Taxus baccata*) is quite long-lived, ranging in possible lifespan from a few hundred years to perhaps even 2,000. Ancient yew trees may be found in churchyards throughout Britain, France and Spain and the yew is associated with the rune Eihwaz, which signifies the mysteries of death and longevity.

See DEATH, LIMINALITY and RUNES.

LA MONTE YOUNG · Minimalist composer and musician, associated with the Fluxus art movement and pioneer of the drone style or genre. Young's compositions are often written in the style of the Fluxus "event scores" used in performance art (which derived conceptually from musical scores in the first place), an example being "draw a straight line and follow it" · simple and abstract, but action oriented. Founder of the Theatre of Eternal Music, also known as the Dream Syndicate (not to be confused with the Paisley Underground band of the same name), Young was an important influence on John Cale, Brian Eno and many others.

See DRONE, ANGUS MACLISE, KARLHEINZ STOCKHAUSEN and VELVET UNDERGROUND.

Z

Z'EV – Performing name of percussionist, poet and qabalist Stefan Joel Weisser. Z'ev is a respected pioneer within the Industrial music genre, though his own formative influences include Dixieland jazz, rock and World music.

Z'ev is known for both his innovative performance style and his Rhythmajik system. In the late 1970s e.v., he began creating industrial assemblages of metal and plastic so as to integrate movement into performances that were visual as well as musical. The Rhythmajik system (explicated in a book of the same name) employs number mysticism to express over 5,000 beat patterns that may be used to facilitate trance, healing and ritual.

See ALCHEMY, ART OF NOISES, INDUSTRIAL CULTURE, JILL PURCE, QABALA and SHAMANISM.

ZOS KIA CULTUS · Creative ethos comprised of the ideas, techniques, writings and artwork put forward by Austin Osman Spare. Not a group or movement of the usual type but a psycho-magical construct or matrix. The name derives from key terms used by Spare in his writing: *Zos* for "Hand" and *Kia* for "Eye" · perfect starting points for a visual artist like Spare.

The Kia is the Eye of that which Perceives, a homonym of "I" and symbol of the essential Self - the "Atmospheric I" - while Zos represents the body as a whole (including the mind) as the hand or instrument of that Self. Spare used the magical name Zos vel Thanatos and made a hermit named Zos the Goatherd the mouthpiece for his extended rant, the *Anathema of Zos*.

The Book of Zos Kia Cultus is *The Book of Pleasure (Self-Love): The Psychology of Ecstasy*. The full name of the *Book of Pleasure* provides clues for its understanding. Self-Love is central: the endless projection of Kia into manifestation, pleasuring itself among all possibilities. Spare provides several technologies in the Book of Pleasure for discovering and enhancing this experience: the state of Neither-Neither, the Death Posture, the Psychology of Belief and Sigils.

The state of Neither-Neither is attained through a form of meditation in which a pair of opposites are alternately contemplated and then as a spectrum rather than a dichotomy. This spectrum will be seen to include a place in the middle, between the two poles, where the thing is neither one nor the other. The Death Posture is a more radical method involving mirror-gazing and hyperventilation to achieve a break in the patterns of mind.

The Psychology of Belief relates to how the Self (Kia) may enhance its experience from this neutral position as it will. Spare advised thinking not just about *what* you believe but also about *how* you believe. The Psychology of Belief is the science of harnessing the power and structure of Belief to manifest new experiences and realities - and, as it echoes the subtitle of the *Book of Pleasure*, we can infer that Ecstasy is the Book's primary value for such manifestations. The contemporary discipline of Neurolinguistic Programming also provides new techniques for working with the Psychology of Belief.

Finally, the Sigil is the most concrete and practical technology presented in the *Book of Pleasure*. Sigils are quite similar to the ancient Germanic practice of creating bind-runes as well as a method given by Cornelius Agrippa. A statement of intent is made concerning a desired magical outcome, repeating letters are eliminated and then the remaining letters are creatively combined into a single glyph.

This glyph is then implanted into the subconscious through either some method such as the Death Posture or by obsession to the point of exhaustion (commonly through orgasm by Magicians today). In either case, the conscious mind is moved out of the way and the Sigil goes to work through the energies of the subconscious. As with the Psychology of Belief, methodologies such as Neurolinguistic Programming or hypnosis, as well as advances in video and audio technology, can be used to enhance work with Sigils.

The Sacraments of Zos Kia Cultus are the Sabbat - where Spirit, Flesh, Time and Place come together in the continuum of Dream - and liminality in general, what Spare called the "Sacred Inbetweenness Concepts". The Law of Zos Kia Cultus is to trespass all laws.

The Creed of Zos Kia Cultus is the Living Flesh, best expressed in the following prayer from the *Anathema of Zos*:

O Self my God, foreign is thy name except in blasphemy, for I am thy iconoclast. I cast thy bread upon the waters, for I myself am meat enough. Hidden in the labyrinth of the Alphabet is my sacred name, the Sigil of all things unknown. On Earth my kingdom is Eternity of Desire. My wish incarnates in the belief and becomes flesh, for, I am the Living Truth. Heaven is ecstacy; my consciousness changing and acquiring association. May I have courage to take from my own superabundance. Let me forget righteousness. Free me of morals. Lead me into temptation of myself, for I am a tottering kingdom of good and evil.

May worth be acquired through those things I have pleasured.

May my trespass be worthy.

Give me the death of my soul. Intoxicate me with self-love. Teach me to sustain its freedom; for I am sufficiently Hell. Let me sin against the small beliefs. -Amen.

See ILLUMINATES OF THANATEROS, LIMINALITY and AUSTIN OSMAN SPARE.

ACKNOWLEDGMENTS

The deepest of thanks to Hannah Haddix, for her practical help and suggestions, encouragement, love, beauty, rarity of mind and general magicalness. And to Matthew Levi Stevens for going through his ancient notebooks and suggesting so many good topics for entries.

Thanks also to Florian Stinglmayr, Charles Becker, Peter Windle, Justin Bradshaw, Lloyd Keane, Peribenset, Cathlain, Jeffrey Richey, Christopher Ballard, Peter Greening, Christopher Athanasiadis and Donki Ra Mansour for their crowdfunding support in the creation of Horngate Media.

Inadequate and humble thanks to John Balance and Peter Christopherson.

And to the Nameless and the Shapeless...

Lightning Source UK Ltd.
Milton Keynes UK
UKHW031451071118
331928UK00004B/486/P